Anita Soni and Sue Bristow

THE
KEY PERSON
APPROACH

Practical ideas to help this work

Published 2012 by Featherstone Education
Bloomsbury Publishing plc
50 Bedford Square, London,
www.acblack.com

ISBN 978-1-4081-3730-7

Text © Anita Soni and Sue Bristow 2012
Design © Lynda Murray
Photographs © Shutterstock

The book is dedicated to the Key People in our lives who have supported us to be able to share our passions with others.

Printed in Great Britain by Latimer Trend & Company Ltd

This book is produced using paper that is made from wood grown in
managed, sustainable forests. It is natural, renewable and recyclable.
The logging and manufacturing processes conform to the environmental
regulations of the country of origin.

To see our full range of titles visit **www.acblack.com**

Contents

2011004089

Key Person Approach

This book has been written because we are very passionate about the importance of the Key Person approach. Everyone, no matter what age, needs key people in their lives. Most of the time, when life coasts along at an even pace, we don't even realise that we need them. However, every so often, in moments of strong emotion – whether we feel very sad, stressed or happy – we all need someone to share our feelings with.

Nowadays, we adults are fortunate in that we can contact those who are close to us quickly, on our mobile phones. If we ever won the lottery, the first people we would want to speak to would be the key people in our lives – partners, parents, children or close friends.

Children are more likely than adults to have moments of strong emotion. Pause and think how many times a day a young child or baby you know feels an emotion strongly. It is likely to be a lot of times, so babies and young children need key people even more than adults do. They need someone at their setting to have a close and warm relationship with, someone to turn to when things get tough and they need help or comfort, and someone to help them learn how to be strong, confident and independent.

This book

This book is aimed at practitioners, managers and teachers who work in early years settings. It is organised into chapters, but it doesn't have to be read in sequence. It is intended to be a practical book that gives relevant background information, but which also promotes reflective practice with regard to the Key Person approach. All the chapters contain key messages, and Chapters 4 to 10 contain audits and self-evaluation activities to support practitioners in reflecting upon their practice.

If you are interested in the literature and research behind the Key Person approach, then please do have a look at Chapter 1. It may be helpful for assignments, or simply to satisfy an interest.

Chapter 2 explains how the Key Person system is utilised in the United Kingdom, with a particular focus on England.

Chapter 3 examines what a Key Person is and is not, and compares it to the key worker – a source of frequent confusion in our experience. This chapter also looks at who benefits from the Key Person approach.

In Chapters 4, 5 and 6, we look at important aspects of using the Key Person method: shared care, secure attachment and independence. Each of these chapters begins by examining why this aspect is so important, and

concludes with activities and questions for you to reflect upon, in order that you can congratulate yourself on good practice and seek to develop this further.

Chapters 7, 8 and 9 consider key issues within early years practice, and how these relate to the Key Person approach. Chapter 7 starts with observation, assessment and planning. Chapter 8 looks at safeguarding and how this needs to be considered alongside the Key Person approach. Chapter 9 looks at thinking critically, as the Key Person is very well placed to support and develop episodes of sustained shared thinking with their key children.

Chapter 10 focuses on the issue of supervision, and how it is important for practitioners to feel supported in being effective and happy Key People.

Chapters 11 and 12 are intended to support settings in developing or enhancing their Key Person approach. They contain activities, case studies and questions to reflect upon, in order to self-evaluate how well the setting is progressing, as well as to recognise and celebrate what is going well and develop this further.

We hope that you find this book useful for your practice. The Key Person approach is not without challenge, but everyone needs a Key Person, especially a young child or baby in an early years setting.

Chapter 1

The theories underpinning the Key Person approach

This chapter explores and explains some of the theories underpinning the Key Person approach. It examines how attachment style can affect a child's development and considers the implications for attachment and the Key Person approach in early years settings.

What is attachment?

Both the *Early Years Learning and Development Review* (Evangelou et al, 2009) and literature review for *Birth to Three Matters* (David et al, 2003) highlight that one of the most important theories of early childhood development for early years practitioners is Bowlby's theory of attachment (1953, 1969, 1973, and 1980).

Bowlby viewed attachment – and linked behaviours such as clinging, crying and staying near an adult – as an adaptive behaviour with an evolutionary basis, since it supported the continuation of the human species.

Within Bowlby's theory, attachment is the development of a strong nurturing bond between mother and child during the first few months of life. By the time the baby reaches seven to nine months, this close bond is well established. Therefore babies of this age will show separation anxiety, by crying and getting unsettled when separated from their primary caregiver, typically the baby's mother.

Ainsworth et al (1978) argue that this first important attachment relationship or close bond serves to provide the child with a secure emotional base that can have a significant bearing on their future emotional and social development. There is a wealth of literature on attachment, and this generally has centred upon the mother-child bond. Such a tight focus on the mother-child bond has often been used as a basis for criticism of the concept; Ainsworth et al. (1978) acknowledged the possibility and importance of other attachment figures in a child's life, such as the father, siblings and extended family.

Trevarthen (1988) further developed the concept of 'intersubjectivity', where the shared understanding between mother and child is achieved through

recognition and coordination of the communication between them. This is achieved by mother and child having a shared focus of attention, and agreement on the nature of how they are going to communicate. In young babies this is likely to be through smiles, gurgles and eye gaze. As the child grows older, language is increasingly used.

Trevarthen focused on the idea of this interplay between mother and child being like a dance, and postulated that babies are active in motivating mothers to interact with them through their natural sociability. Trevarthen extends the idea of attachment by stating that mothers go beyond being a secure base for their babies, and play the role of friend and playmate.

The Early Years Foundation Stage (EYFS) (DCSF, 2008a) defines attachment within the glossary:

> 'Attachment behaviour is shown when babies and young children actively seek close relationships with their parents and other primary caregivers.'

This definition focuses on the role of attachment within families, but does extend the idea to primary caregivers, though not explicitly to those beyond the home.

The Personal, Social and Emotional Development (PSED) training materials (Sure Start, 2006) explain attachment in the following way:

> 'All humans have an inbuilt desire to form an intense emotional tie with a close caregiver. This helps to ensure survival, provides care and nurture and gives a sense of security. These ties, or attachments, influence the way babies and young children feel secure, explore and learn about the world around them, and how they seek help and comfort. The way in which these close emotional ties develop becomes the blueprint for the comfort, care and closeness that babies and young children expect from other important relationships.'

This definition acknowledges Bowlby's idea of attachment as an adaptive behaviour which helps to promote survival. It builds upon this, to explain that attachment has an impact on how children feel about themselves and others, and also on how they learn.

However, it is important to recognise that this emotional tie can vary across cultures and within different patterns of care. Children of differing backgrounds and experiences will have a range of emotional relationships. These relationships change over time as the needs of the child alters. So as the child grows older, the emotional tie gradually becomes more of a partnership in which ideas, feelings and plans are negotiated and shared.

What is secure attachment?

The PSED training materials (Sure Start, 2006) use three building blocks for the three aspects of being close:

→ Feeling secure

→ Separating and exploring

→ Seeking help and comfort

These materials explain secure attachment in the following way. When babies and young children feel secure, they are more at ease and content. Once at ease, they feel more able and confident to show interest and explore the world around them. At the same time, they feel safe in the knowledge that there is someone to whom they can turn when comfort and reassurance is needed.

This may be similar to how you might feel in a strange place or situation, such as a new job or a party. Once you have familiarised yourself with a new environment – where things are, and how things work – you begin to relax, and feel more able to chat and talk to others and find out what is going on. However it helps to have a friend or partner close by, who you can turn back to when it all gets a bit too challenging!

Feeling secure

The building block 'Feeling secure' is needed as it enables children to be open and interested in the world around them, and then to venture into it, to learn and discover. It gives children the security that they will be helped when they need it, cared for and comforted when upset, and provides a sense of reassurance and confidence. It also helps children to cope with the emotional demands of unfamiliar activities and experiences (which may be exciting but can seem a bit overwhelming) by themselves, without their parents/carers.

By comparison, children who feel insecure may feel very anxious and troubled by being separated from parents/carers or they may seem unusually unconcerned or even lost. Such children are unable to explore the world around them and the exciting opportunities within it. In the early days at a new setting, a child who has the building block of 'Feeling secure' at home is likely to be anxious about separation from their important people at home. A child who has been settled at an early years setting and has built up the building block of 'Feeling secure', but then has a long period of time off, will also need time to build up that block again and may well be upset about being separated from their parents/carers.

Separating and exploring

The building block 'Separating and exploring' is needed as the Key Person has to provide a two-part balancing act. On the one hand, as the practitioner you need to give children a sense of security, but on the other hand you have to encourage, reassure and keep an eye on children in order to allow them to explore and engage with the activities and experiences in the setting. This can be challenging, as the child's need for security and comfort has to be carefully balanced with encouragement to explore and find things out alone.

This is a gradual process from birth to five, and needs to be made manageable and safe for each child, depending on their stage of development. It begins with the Key Person being closely involved, offering interesting and attractive interaction and activities to babies. As the child finds that being separate from their Key Person becomes more manageable, they can be encouraged to explore and discover interesting environments, where they can choose and carry out their own activities and learn through trial and error. This requires an early years environment where the boundaries and rules are clear in order to keep children safe, but importantly where independent learning is valued and encouraged.

The Key Person needs to plan and act carefully when encouraging separation and discovery in babies and young children who feel insecure and uneasy, showing respect for their feelings when they need comfort or security. This means going at the child's pace rather than the Key Person's pace, building the child's confidence, and supporting their learning. You may have to provide additional help and encouragement to children who find it difficult to build close emotional ties with other staff. This is discussed further in Chapter 6.

Seeking help and comfort

The building block 'Seeking help and comfort' is needed because all babies and young children will have times where they feel unsettled, distressed and overwhelmed. When this happens, whatever the age of the child, there must be a Key Person to turn to for comfort and help. Think of a time when you have been upset such as receiving some difficult news or being upset by someone. More than likely you wanted to turn to your own close friends or relations for help and comfort. If you are unable to obtain help and comfort by telephone or in person, you will probably remain upset for longer.

This is the same for children. However, as a child gets older and becomes more aware of their own feelings and better able to communicate, they will be able to show when they need help and comfort. Children with a warm, nurturing Key Person relationship will feel more able to turn for help and comfort, confident in the knowledge that they will be understood and their needs taken care of.

You need to be willing to respond to children in need of comfort and help, and to know the different ways in which individual babies and children like to be helped, comforted and reassured. Some babies and young children will need more help than others; some may not look for it enough, and might need encouragment to do so. The many different ways of giving soothing attention – the calming tone, the words of comfort and the way of holding, rocking, stroking and patting – will vary from child to child and will change over time.

The early years environment needs to contain a quiet space where children can be consoled and calmed down – perhaps a cosy space with gentle music and comforting drinks. When they are able, children need the chance to explain what has happened and to talk about how they feel.

The Social and Emotional Aspects of Development guidance (DCSF, 2008b) explains that babies are vulnerable and totally dependent on others for survival. They need to have what is called a 'secure attachment'. These materials explain that a child with secure attachment feels able to rely on their parents or Key Person for safety and comfort, and uses these important attachment relationships as bases from which to explore and learn about the world.

What are the other types of attachment?

The PSED training materials (Sure Start, 2006) remind us that, while the majority of children develop secure attachments, there are a small number of children who may develop insecure emotional ties or attachments. Such children do not easily feel secure or comforted by the person to whom they are attached, and are more likely to find it difficult to manage their feelings and behaviour.

Insecure and avoidant attachment

A child is likely to become rather solitary, distant and unfriendly when their caregiver persistently ignores their distress and fails to respond to their feelings, and so may develop an 'insecure and avoidant attachment'. As a result the child may pay little attention to the person to whom they are attached, and appear to deal with separations well. The child has learned a way of coping with strong emotions that is unhelpful – they have learned not to display their strong emotions as they have not received comfort and help when they have needed it.

Insecure and uncertain attachment

On the other hand, children who have experience of adults who care for them in a very anxious and overprotective way can become very distressed, fearful and difficult to settle when separated. Here, the child is almost led to believe that they need comfort and help at all times. Such children are unable to explore on their own, as they have not been reassured and encouraged to do so when they are feeling secure. Such children – who tend to be clingy, unhappy and over reliant on others – may develop an 'insecure and uncertain attachment'.

Insecure and confused attachment

An even smaller number of children, usually as a result of very difficult experiences early in life, display their insecurity by becoming very unpredictable and unsettled. They can, at times, display unusual behaviour, such as wanting to be close but simultaneously hitting out, or looking for closeness and comfort from strangers. Such children may develop an 'insecure and confused attachment'.

A child who develops an insecure attachment should still be supported, in order that they might develop secure attachments within their early years setting. The literature on resilience indicates that it is important for babies and young children to have opportunities in which to build early secure relationships and such opportunities do not have to be solely in the home.

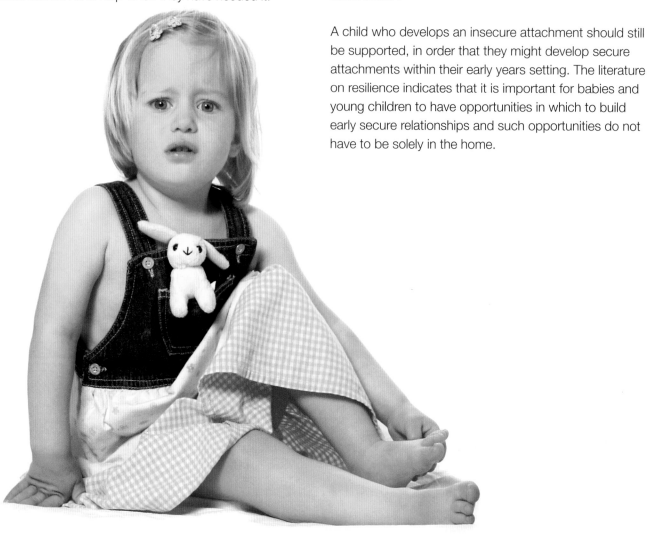

How does secure attachment affect a child's development?

The impact of a secure attachment between mother and baby has been linked to a range of different outcomes for a child in their social and emotional development, including:

- **early conscience development**
  (Laible and Thompson, 2000)

- **emotional understanding**
  (Kochanska, 2001; De Rosnay and Harris, 2002)

- **pro-social understandings and self-regulation**
  (Kochanska, 2002; Kochanska et al., 2004).

This highlights how important early childhood attachments are for children's development, both socially and emotionally.

The importance of adults being responsive and building upon children's interactions is evident in accounts of a child's emotional development. Robinson (2003) emphasises that emotional warmth from adults is even more powerful when it is genuinely responsive to the child's own emotions in the child's first year of life. She also stresses the importance of familiar adults being present and understanding the child's routine. Laible and Thompson (2000), commenting on recent literature regarding early socialisation, also support the influence of children having a warm and mutually responsive relationship with adults. They emphasise the importance of structure for young children, as this allows them to feel that they have control and there is predictability in their days.

Authors such as Gerhardt (2004) and the National Scientific Council on the Developing Child (2007) make striking claims about the importance of children's early emotional experiences on how their brains develop and are shaped. The National Scientific Council on the Developing Child identifies that the architecture of the brain depends on the influences of genetics, environment and experience, and that early environments and experiences have a remarkably strong influence on the brain.

Gerhardt suggests that some cognitive processes are dependent on the development of emotional processes, and that caregivers need to identify with the children they look after. The National Scientific Council on the Developing Child calls the period of exceptional sensitivity to the effects of the environment and experience 'a sensitive period' and states that these sensitive periods occur at different ages for different parts of the brain.

Gerhardt suggests that the neural connections within the brain are significantly related to emotional experiences, particularly within the six to twelve months age period, when different regions of the brain are particularly impacted by socio-emotional experiences. She argues that early experiences establish the physiological patterns of emotional response within a child's brain, and may even impact on the formation of important structures within the brain, such as the hippocampus. This is part of the limbic system and is thought to have an important role in relation to memory and emotion.

Gerhardt argues that from the third year of a child's life, the hippocampus begins to play a key role in the regulation of stress. So early emotional experiences may have an irreversible impact on a child's subsequent ability to manage and respond to stress. Gerhardt therefore places a very high value on the importance of the development of secure early relationships for children. The National Scientific Council on the Developing Child agrees that impoverished early experiences can have a severe and long-lasting effect on later brain development. However, brain development is viewed as less fixed and irreversible. It is emphasised that brain plasticity continues throughout life, and therefore later intervention is feasible but is likely to be harder, more expensive in terms of effort and potentially less durable.

Thompson (2000) emphasises that it is vital to understand that attachment security is dynamic and can change. Thompson argues that attachment should not be viewed as having to be attained within a certain critical time period, that is, within the child's first year. Instead, attachment might more usefully be thought of as developing as the child grows older, and changing as the child understands more about the people around them. Such changes in understanding might occur due to specific events, such as the arrival of a new baby, or could occur more generally as the developing child experiences different social relationships, and mixes with a range of children.

While Belsky and Fearon (2002) reinforce the importance of early secure attachment for a range of outcomes, they also found that early insecure attachment can actually be counterbalanced by later, highly sensitive mothering. This would suggest that a child's later, positive experiences of secure relationships can moderate the effects of earlier insecure relationships. This is important for early years practitioners, as it shows that attachment relationships at the setting may be extremely helpful and supportive to children who have early insecure attachments. This is discussed further in the following section on resilience.

How does attachment affect resilience?

David et al. (2003) describe resilience as the extent to which 'some children are able to overcome the effects of negative events or experiences'. Roberts (2010) cites Johnson and Howard (1999) in defining resilient children:

> 'They are the ones who are being described as "resilient" because they seem to have an ability to hang on in there when the going gets tough.'

The concept of resilience is important, as it helps us consider how much a child may be able to thrive and overcome challenging parts of their lives. Roberts also reminds us that all children are exposed to the 'normal' adversities of childhood to a certain degree, and that no child really lives life without facing a challenge or difficulty at some time.

The security of a child's attachment has been linked to the developing, and long-term, sense of self and resilience. This means that how a child views themselves (both as a child and on into adulthood) is affected by the security of their relationships. David et al (2003) concluded that a key factor which enabled children to overcome life's challenges was the presence of at least one 'very nurturing relationship'. It is important to note that this one relationship does not have to be with a parent; a child might have strong attachments both within the family and within their early years setting.

An important US longitudinal study, *The Minnesota Study of Risk and Adaptation from Birth to Adulthood* (Sroufe et al., 2005), followed 180 children born into poverty from birth onwards. The study concluded that resilience in the face of adversity was not some 'magical quality' within the children themselves but was due to children having 'a positive platform or balancing supports available later'. This indicates that the early years are an important period of development, and the positive platform refers to early experiences with carers at home and beyond. Sroufe et al add that the presence of balancing supports beyond early childhood can also re-balance the negative effects of early adverse environments such as poverty.

A potential to overcome early deprivation – to exhibit resilience – has also been demonstrated in studies of Romanian children, who experienced severe deprivation in care institutions in Romania during the 1990s. The children were subsequently adopted into UK homes (Rutter et al., 2007). It is potentially significant that the adoptions occurred relatively early in their lives, before the age of three and a half years, follow-up studies at ages four, six and eleven show 'marked catch-up' in their psychological well-being. This 'catch-up' did vary relative to individual temperament. This again highlights the importance of secure relationships in the early years of life.

How does it affect a child to attend an early years setting?

The outcomes for children who attend early years settings, rather than having family-based care, is an important but controversial topic. In the USA, the National Institute of Child Health and Human Development (NICHD) Study of Early Child Care has followed over 1000 children from birth through to school age. Belsky et al. (2007) report that children attending early childcare benefit from attaining higher linguistic and cognitive outcomes. However, this is only one part of the picture. The studies also found a link between longer periods in childcare and teacher-reported risks of externalising (anti-social and aggressive) behaviours in children, when they reached school starting age. This latter effect diminished in later years, and was affected by the quality and type of childcare experienced. Indeed, the NICHD study report (Belsky, 2006) states:

'Children who were exclusively cared for by their mothers did not develop differently than those who were also cared for by others.'

Within the UK, there are similar findings in the *Effective Provision of Preschool Education* (EPPE) study (Sylva et al., 2008). It was found that attending pre-schools had positive effects on children's linguistic and cognitive development, but that the social outcomes of pre-school education were found to be less beneficial for some children. This is particularly so for boys in socially disadvantaged circumstances.

However, an important element of the EPPE study, and related Researching Effective Pedagogy in the Early Years (REPEY) findings (Siraj-Blatchford et al., 2002), is the significance of adult/child relationships as an indicator of quality within the most effective settings. A high quality setting was signified by high quality relationships between adults and children. This resonates with the NICHD study (1996), which noted that staff who were 'more educated' and 'held more child-centred beliefs about childrearing' were more likely to have positive relationships with the children they cared for.

Does it matter that a child has a new attachment relationship in their early years setting?

In reviewing the literature on attachment relationships beyond the traditional mother-child bond, Howes (1999) states that the key determinants as to whether a child forms a bond with non-maternal caregivers (those who provide care but are not the child's mother) include:

1. whether the caregiver provides both physical and emotional care

2. whether that person is a consistent presence within the child's social network

3. whether the caregiver has an emotional investment in the child.

Although this research is based on those who give care to children beyond mothers, there are some important messages for practitioners who work with young children and babies. Within early years settings, which provide care and education outside the family, there needs to be a consistent early years practitioner who is with the child for stable periods of time. Such practice will create a predictable pattern in interactions. This Key Person needs to provide physical care for the child, and to invest in the child at an emotional level. This is further discussed in Chapter 4.

The PSED training materials (Sure Start, 2006) remind practitioners that having a Key Person in the setting remains compatible with the concept of parents having a strong warm attachment with their child at home, and is needed by every child in the setting:

> 'A close emotional tie with a key person in an early years setting does not undermine a child's secure attachment with their parent. In fact, every baby and young child needs to build such a relationship in their setting to feel safe and sound as well as feel confident to learn and develop. A key person needs to be able to develop a genuine bond with a child and to offer a settled, close relationship in which they can provide warm, sensitive care readily and willingly so that all babies and young children can find comfort and support when needed.'

One close relationship does not threaten the stability or the closeness of the other relationship. An ideal start in life is where a child has strong, secure relationships both at home and in the setting.

How can attachment theory be reinforced in early years settings?

One way of reflecting the importance of emotional warmth and security for young children has been to recommend the appointment of 'Key Persons' within settings (Elfer, Goldschmied and Selleck, 2003). In this way, specific practitioners are linked to specific children. Elfer et al describe the Key Person approach as:

> '...a way of working in nurseries in which the whole focus and organisation is aimed at enabling and supporting close attachments between individual children and individual staff. The Key Person approach is an involvement, an individual and reciprocal commitment between a member of staff and a family.'

When attending an early years setting, a child who feels secure will be able to form a close, successful relationship with a Key Person. This Person is defined by the EYFS (DCSF 2008a) as a practitioner who has special responsibilities for working with a small number of children, and building relationships with their parents.

Such children will display the three building blocks of being close. They will feel secure in the early years setting, will enjoy their growing independence and be able to separate, explore and learn with confidence, yet will be aware that they can turn to their Key Person when upset and in need of help or comfort. For this to happen, babies and children need to build a special close emotional relationship with one, or maybe two, key people in their setting. The Key Person should be able to form warm, settled, emotionally close relationships with the children concerned. However, closeness is not just about seeking help and comfort when distressed or uncomfortable; there is a value in enjoyable, shared, special time so that babies and young children can continue to build and reinforce the special relationship with their Key Person.

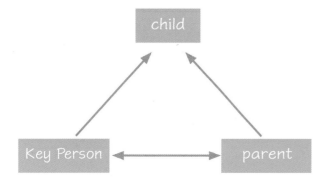

The Key Person approach does, of course, have challenges. Staff might need support in order to manage the needs of their key children compared to other children in the group, and children and parents will need support if their Key Person leaves or is on extended absence. These issues are discussed further in Chapter 11. There are emotional implications for practitioners, families and children when a Key Person forges close emotional ties to particular children. Elfer and Dearnley (2007) therefore argue for there to be continuing professional development for staff. This should deal with supporting the emotional needs of young children and of themselves as professionals. The issue of support for practitioners and supervision is discussed in Chapter 10.

What kind of positive relationships should be developed by a Key Person?

The research evidence in the Early Years Learning and Development Review (Evangelou et al, 2009) identifies the following key aspects of relationships:

- **the warmth of relationships**

- **the contingency of relationships**

- **the use of talk in building and maintaining such relationships**

- **the recognition of the uniqueness and agency of the child** (the feeling that the child can make a difference to their own life and to others)

- **the importance of mutually responsive relationships in facilitating pro-social thinking and behaviour.**

A child's social and emotional development is enhanced by secure attachment with at least one Key Person who identifies with them strongly. The characteristics of these warm nurturing relationships are that the Key Person is responsive both to the child and the parents, giving regular, supportive feedback to the parents and supporting the child in their care routines. Familiarity with, and the presence of, a caring Key Person provides the child with a safe and secure environment in the setting. Children of all ages need opportunities to have their feelings recognised, and responded to, by their Key Person. The children also need to have positive

conversations with their Key Person. This supports both the development of a child's self-esteem and their understanding of what is expected in the setting. This in turn helps children to develop their abilities to respond socially and emotionally to others.

As well as recognising and responding to the child's key relationships with their parents/carers, it is important for a Key Person to remember the role of others in a child's world, such as siblings and extended family. As the child grows older, the Key Person needs to be able to discuss a child's friendships with them, as these become increasingly important to children through the early years.

The Key Person needs to demonstrate 'attunement' to their key children. This means that the adult is able to respond in a speedy and appropriate manner to the child's communication. For example, if a child is crying because she wants some comfort, the Key Person recognises that need quickly and is able to respond in the way the child prefers best. However, if a child is in need of encouragement to play and explore, a Key Person is able to recognise and support that need equally. A high level of contingent responses by the Key Person helps the child to:

- **gain a sense of self during their first year**

- **understand their social world and what is expected of them**

- **socialise with others within particular contexts.**

It is important for the development of a child's understanding of themselves and others that the responses of the Key Person are underpinned by warmth and positivity. However, while the Key Person's responses to the child should be receptive to the child's desires and behaviours, the responses may change in different contexts, or as the child changes. For instance, the Key

Person may respond to the child's needs immediately when they are very young, or new to the setting, but later may help the child to wait for a few moments.

Roberts (2010) identifies five principles of companionable learning with which to support children's well-being, which are very relevant to the Key Person approach. These are:

- **companionable attention** – the child getting the full attention of their Key Person

- **agency in companionable play** – the child is given the idea that they can make a difference to, and have some control of, their play with the Key Person

- **anchored attention** – the child knows that they have guaranteed times where they enjoy the companionable and full attention of their Key Person, and further that they are kept in the Key Person's mind

- **companionable apprenticeship** – children being active companions in everyday, real tasks where they can help

- **a child's personal time and space** – going at the pace of the child, allowing them sufficient time to do or think about things.

Rich communication between the child and the Key Person supports children in building relationships with adults and with other children. This communication can come in many forms, and includes response to body language and gestures as much as to the spoken word. Rich conversations about feelings with their Key Person enhance a child's self-esteem and emotional understanding. These conversations can stem from stories, pretend play, or real-life contexts. They help to promote trusting relationships which in turn build a child's emotional awareness and self-regulation. Such conversations can also demonstrate appropriate ways of expressing emotions and behaviours. Research suggests that the most effective conversations have an 'elaborative narrative style' that goes beyond a description, and allows the child time to reflect on experiences and hypothesise about what else could happen. This is expanded upon in Chapter 9 on Thinking Critically.

How is the child seen within the Key Person approach?

Within the Key Person approach, the child is recognised as playing an active rather than a passive part in their own development. Each child has to be recognised as being unique, with an individual temperament; equally, each Key Person is unique. This results in each child experiencing a different pattern of relationships, and displaying different social behaviours and interactions, both at home and in the setting.

The choice of who should be a child's Key Person within a setting is important, and needs consideration and consultation with all involved. It should also be acknowledged that the selection of a Key Person cannot always remain the same, and may change as the child develops and changes.

Children's socialisation is best supported within a 'social relational model'. Here, a child's thinking about relationships and behaviour is facilitated by the child internalising rules through a mutually responsive relationship between themselves and their Key Person, rather than having rules set by staff about their behaviour. This mutual responsiveness by the Key Person; rich conversations about how the child is feeling, combined with discussion on social behaviour, helps to shape the development of conscience. This helps to promote positive behaviour and compliance with the social rules of the setting, since the child will understand and wish to behave in the way encouraged by their Key Person – whether they are present or not. Clearly, this is preferable to superficial compliance, where the child does as asked but only when the adult is present.

Key messages

Remember that:

- An attachment is shown when babies and young children seek warm, close relationships with their parents and other primary caregivers, such as their Key Person.

- Building a secure attachment is made up of three parts that help the child feel secure, separate and explore, and seek help and comfort when needed.

- Children may develop different types of attachment, with the majority of children developing secure attachments.

- The importance of a secure attachment has been linked to a child's social and emotional development.

- A key factor that enables children to be resilient is the presence of at least one nurturing, close relationship in the child's life.

- High quality settings are signified by warm, responsive relationships between adults and children that recognise the individuality of the child.

- Babies and young children can have a few close relationships; the relationship with a Key Person does not affect other close relationships with the family.

- A child needs a close warm relationship with a Key Person, to enable them to feel secure in each setting they attend.

The Key Person approach in the United Kingdom

This chapter looks at the way in which the Key Person approach can be found in the UK curricula. These include:

* ***The Early Years Foundation Stage*** (DCSF, 2008a) and (DfE 2012) for England

* ***Pre-Birth to Three Positive Outcomes for Scotland's Children and Families*** (Learning and Teaching Scotland, 2010)

* ***A Framework for Children's Learning for 3-7 year olds in Wales*** (Welsh Assembly Government, 2008a)

* ***Curricular Guidance for Pre-School Education*** (Northern Ireland Council for the Curriculum, Examinations and Assessment, 2006) and the Foundation Stage in Northern Ireland.

England

The Early Years Foundation Stage (EYFS) was a central part of the Childcare Act 2006 and was intended to improve outcomes for children and reduce inequalities between different group of children. The Childcare Act 2006 gave legal force to the EYFS in September 2008, and became mandatory for all schools and early years providers in OFSTED registered settings attended by children aged from birth to the end of the academic year in which the child is five years old.

The EYFS has been revised and updated in March 2012, and these revisions are to be implemented by September 2012. The reformed EYFS is intended to reduce paperwork and bureaucracy, further strengthen partnerships between parents and professionals,

focus on the three prime areas of learning most essential to children's readiness for future learning and healthy development, simplify assessment at the age of five and provide for early intervention where needed through the introduction of a progress check at the age of two (Overall reforms to the 2012 EYFS Framework, 2012). The revised materials include:

● **Updated EYFS Profile guidance**

● **Remodelled 'Development Matters' material (Early Education, 2012)**

● **New Statutory Framework for the EYFS (DfE, 2012)**

● **A summary of the EYFS for parents**

● **2 year old progress check guidance (NCB, 2012)**

The remodelled Development Matters in the EYFS (Early Education, 2012) replaces the previous Practice Guidance for the EYFS (DCSF, 2008a). The new Statutory Framework for the EYFS (DfE 2012) replaces the previous version (DCSF, 2008a). However the guidance on implementing the new EYFS states '…there are NO changes to the principles and commitments in the 2012 EYFS Framework posters and cards' (Foundation Years website, 2012) and encourages use of these for reflection.

The Key Person approach and the Statutory Framework for the EYFS (DfE, 2012)

The Statutory Framework for the EYFS (DFE, 2012) sets out what the EYFS seeks to provide;

- **Quality and consistency in all early years settings, so that every child makes good progress and no child gets left behind;**

- **A secure foundation through learning and development opportunities which are planned around the needs and interests of each individual child and are assessed and reviewed regularly;**

- **Partnership working between practitioners and with parents and/or carers;**

- **Equality of opportunity and anti-discriminatory practice, ensuring that every child is included and supported. (page 2, DfE, 2012)**

The Statutory Framework for the EYFS (DfE 2012) specifies:

- **the learning and development requirements (the seven areas of learning and development and the educational programmes, the early learning goals and the assessment arrangements)**

- **the safeguarding and welfare requirements (steps providers must take to keep children safe and promote their welfare)**

The learning and development requirements are given legal force by an Order made under Section 39 (1) (a) of the Childcare Act 2006. The safeguarding and welfare requirements are given legal force under Section 39 (1) (b) of the Childcare Act 2006.

The Key Person approach plays a key role in the requirements of the Statutory Framework for the EYFS (DfE 2012).

Within the learning and development requirements, the Statutory Framework for the EYFS (DfE 2012) states:

> 'Each child must be assigned a key person. Providers must inform parents and/or carers of the name of the key person, and explain their role, when a child starts attending a setting. The key person must help ensure that every child's learning and care is tailored to meet their individual needs. The key person must seek to engage and support parents and/or carers in guiding their child's development at home. They should also help families engage with more specialist support if appropriate.' (page 7, DfE 2012)

Here the Statutory Framework reminds the practitioner of the role of the key person in terms of relationships with the child and parent/carer rather than being a paperwork or administrative role. Indeed one of the key aims of the reforms of the EYFS is to reduce paperwork and bureaucracy.

Within the safeguarding and welfare requirements, the Statutory Framework for the EYFS (DfE, 2012) states:

> 'Each child must be assigned a key person. Their role is to help ensure that every child's care is tailored to meet their individual needs, to help the child become familiar with the setting, offer a settled relationship for the child and build a relationship with the parents.'
> (page 18, DfE, 2012).

Similarly within the safeguarding and welfare requirement, the key person role is seen as valuable to individualise the child's experiences, help the child feel settled and to build relationships with the parents.

The reformed EYFS (DfE, 2012) has gone further in stating the role of the key person than in the previous version (DCSF, 2008a) where previously:

> 'Each child must be assigned a key person. In childminder settings, the childminder is the key person.' (DCSF, 2008a)

However the guidance that ran alongside this requirement was similar to the phrasing in the reformed EYFS.

The Key Person and Development Matters in the Early Years Foundation Stage (EYFS) (Early Education, 2012)

Development Matters in the EYFS is non-statutory guidance material intended to support practitioners in implementing the statutory requirements of the EYFS. The reformed EYFS has seven areas of learning and development with three being viewed as prime areas: Communication and language, Physical development and Personal, social and emotional development. The four specific areas are; literacy, mathematics, understanding the world and expressive arts and design.

Within the guidance, key person is included under the practice within the theme 'Positive relationships'. It states that;

'Positive relationships are..... built on key person relationships in early years settings.'

Whilst this is not as central as in the positive relationships principle within the Practice Guidance for the EYFS (DCSF, 2008a), there is still an emphasis on the central role the key person plays in babies and young children's lives.

Development Matters in the EYFS gives guidance within each area of learning. Within the prime area of Personal, social and emotional development (PSED), there are a range of statements that relate to the role of the key person. These include:

'Make sure babies have their own special person in the setting, who knows them really well and understands their wants and needs.' (Birth-11 months/8-20 months, PSED: Making relationships)

'Ensure that the key person or buddy is available to greet a young baby at the beginning of the session, and to hand them over to parents at the end of the session, so the young baby is supported and communication with parents is maintained. ' (Birth-11 months/8-20 months, PSED: Making relationships)

'Ensure the key person is paired with a 'buddy' who knows the boy and family as well, and can step in when necessary.' (Birth-11 months/8-20 months, PSED: Making relationships)

'Enable children to explore by providing a secure base for them.' (16-26 months, PSED: Making relationships)

'Make time for children to be with their key person, individually and in their key group.' (22-36 months, PSED: Making relationships)

'Provide stability in staffing, key person relationships and in grouping of the children.' (30-50 months, PSED: Making relationships)

'Ensure children have opportunities to relate to their key person, individually and in small groups.' (40-60 months, PSED: Making relationships)

Whilst these statements are all within PSED: Making relationships, they demonstrate the need for the key person throughout the age range, from birth to the end of the academic year the child is five.

There are other references to the key person within PSED in self-confidence and self-awareness, such as;

'Make sure the child can explore from the secure, close-by presence of their key person.' (16-26 months, PSED: Self-confidence and self-awareness)

'Ensure that key practitioners offer extra support to children in new situations.' (22-36 months/30-50 months, PSED: Self-confidence and self-awareness)

There are also references within PSED in managing feelings and behaviour such as;

'Provide comfortable seating such as a sofa or cushions for baby and key person to be together.' (Birth-11 months, PSED: Managing feelings and behaviour)

'Make sure the key person stays close by and provides a secure presence and a refuge at times a child may be feeling anxious.' (8-20 months, PSED: Managing feelings and behaviour)

These statements reinforce that the key person plays a vital role within Making relationships, but that this role continues across Personal, social and emotional development (PSED) as a whole. There are fewer direct references to the key person role in the rest of the Development Matters guidance, however many of the areas of learning and development encourage reference back to PSED thereby encouraging recognition of the role of the Key Person.

The Key Person approach and the EYFS poster (DCSF, 2008a)

Within the Statutory Framework for the EYFS (DfE 2012) the principle for Positive relationships has changed to:

'Children learn to be strong and independent through **positive relationships**.'

This reflects a change in phrasing from the principles as detailed on the poster which stated:

'Children learn to be strong and independent from a base of loving and secure relationships with parents and/or a key person.' (DSCF, 2008a)

However the message for the need for the key person is in place within the Statutory Framework for the EYFS (DfE 2012) as previously discussed, and the poster and cards are considered useful for reflection (Foundation Years website, 2012).

The Key person approach and the EYFS Principle into Practice Cards (DCSF, 2008a)

On the reverse of the summary Principles into Practice card is the Key Person commitment:

'A key person has special responsibilities for working with a small number of children, giving them the reassurance to feel safe and cared for and building relationships with their parents.'

This emphasises that the role of the Key Person is to work with a number of children and their parents. The use of the word 'small' confirms that the Key Person should have a limited number of children and parents to work with effectively.

The commitment also highlights the responsibilities of the Key Person as:

- **giving reassurance to their key children**

- **enabling their key children to feel safe**

- **supporting the care of their key children**

- **building relationships with their key children's parents.**

Principles into Practice card 2.4: Key Person (DCSF, 2008a)

This card expands further on the commitment. We look at ways to develop the three most important aspects of this commitment in the following chapters:

- **shared care** (Chapter 4)

- **secure attachment** (Chapter 5)

- **independence** (Chapter 6).

The back of the card:

- **provides examples of effective practice from across the age range**

- **recognises common challenges and dilemmas that may result**

- **gives some ideas for reflecting on practice.**

The Foundation Years website notes an expectation that many providers will have a key person system in place, but suggests using the card 2.4 Key Person to reflect on the effectiveness of the key person system, and how well this works for children and families. The commitment from the card, the details on how to promote secure attachment, and the challenges and dilemmas are highlighted.

The highlighted details on how to promote secure attachment are:

'The key person has a special role in supporting attachment.

- A key person helps the baby or child to become familiar with the setting and to feel confident and safe within it.

- A key person develops a genuine bond with children and offers a settled, close relationship.

- When children feel happy and secure in this way they are confident to explore and to try out new things.

- Even when children are older and can hold special people in mind for longer there is still a need for them to have a key person to depend on in the setting, such as their teacher or a teaching assistant' (Foundation Years website, 2012).

This again reinforces the messages within the Statutory Framework for the EYFS (DfE, 2012) and the Development Matters guidance (Early Education, 2012). These are that the key person approach is needed to help a child settle and feel confident, the importance of this and that this is needed across the age range from birth to the academic year when the child is five years old.

The challenges and dilemmas are:

- **Reassuring others that children will not become too dependent on a key person or find it difficult to adjust to being a member of a group.**

- **Meeting children's needs for a key person while being concerned for staff who may feel over-attached to a child.**

- **Reassuring parents who may be concerned that children may be more attached to staff than to them.**

- **Supporting children's transitions within and beyond a setting, particularly as children reach four or five years of age.**

The high number of references and discussion of the key person role within the reformed EYFS (DfE 2012) show this to be a central part of the approach to early years care and education in England. These references have continued from the previous version of the EYFS (DCSF 2008a) showing a continuation of a belief in the importance of the key person role.

Scotland

The document *Pre-Birth to Three: Positive Outcomes for Scotland's Children and Families* replaces *Birth to Three: Supporting our Youngest Children* (Learning and Teaching Scotland 2005). It reflects the principles and philosophies of prevention and early intervention that underpin:

- **The Early Years Framework**
  (Scottish Government, 2008a)

- **Achieving our Potential**
  (Scottish Government, 2008b)

- **Equally Well**
  (Scottish Government, 2008c).

Pre-Birth to Three is intended to lay a secure foundation for children before they engage with the *Curriculum for Excellence 3-18*. It utilises the approaches advocated in *Getting it Right for Every Child* (Scottish Government, 2008d) which states that service providers have to work meaningfully with parents. This entails the adoption of flexible and individualised approaches, recognising the contribution of the family and the children themselves. It was founded on research from Growing Up in Scotland (GUS), funded by the Scottish government and carried out by the Scottish Centre for Social Research (ScotCen), which tracked a representative sample of over 1000 children.

Key principles

The guidance *Pre-Birth to Three* has four key principles:

- **rights of the child**
- **relationships**
- **responsive care**
- **respect.**

The principle of relationships recognises the importance of developing companionable relationships between the staff and children, allowing the children to feel secure, loved and anchored. The ability of the practitioner to anchor children (Roberts, 2010) or in other words to demonstrate to the child, that they are being kept in mind by their Key Person (Elfer et al, 2003) is effective practice. The Key Person approach is identified as an important aspect in establishing the principle of responsive care. The guidance states:

> 'In many early years settings, a clearly defined key person system enables staff to build close, one-to-one, reciprocal relationships with young children and members of their family.'

There are nine effective features of practice to support the implementation of the four key principles. These are:

- **role of staff**
- **attachments**
- **transitions**
- **observation, assessment and planning**
- **partnership working**
- **health and well-being**
- **literacy and numeracy**
- **environments**
- **play.**

The Key Person role

The Key Person is discussed within the 'role of staff' feature, and a detailed description of the role is provided:

> 'The key person meets the needs of every child in their care and responds sensitively to their feelings, ideas and behaviour. They offer security, reassurance and continuity, and are usually responsible for feeding, changing and comforting the child. The key person helps children to develop relationships with members of staff and other children. They skillfully observe children in their play, their relationships, their day-to-day activities, in order to inform future opportunities and experiences that best meet the needs and interests of children. The key person system also enables informed and sensitive communication with the child, family and other agencies, in line with the key components embedded within the Getting it Right approach.'

The *Pre-Birth to Three* guidance has utilised both Robert's (2010) ideas of anchoring, and the Key Person approach as advocated within the EYFS. While the Key Person approach is not mentioned explicitly within the 'attachments' feature of practice, the conceptual ideas of attachment and attunement have clear links to it. The Key Person approach is mentioned within the 'planning' feature of practice, and is stated to be valuable in supporting an approach to planning that is responsive to children's needs, dispositions, interests and stages of development. An effective Key Person who knows his/her key children and their families can best ensure that discussions and decisions about needs and next steps are appropriate.

Guidance materials

A Curriculum for Excellence (Scottish Executive, 2004) sets out the values, purposes and principles for the curriculum for children aged three to eighteen in Scotland. Guidance was originally written in 2006 and was aimed at teachers. Additional guidance, Building the Curriculum Guidance 2010 explicitly goes beyond teachers to include pre-school practitioners. The purpose of the Curriculum for Excellence is to ensure all young people become:

- **successful learners**

- **confident individuals**

- **effective contributors**

- **responsible citizens.**

The *Building the Curriculum* guidance recognises the value of positive health and well-being. The value of creating a climate of trust between learners and teachers is advocated. This is to be developed through positive, open and honest relationships, which enable the children and young people to feel comfortable and secure in offering their own views and ideas.

Building the Curriculum 2: Active Learning in the Early Years (Scottish Executive, 2007) is aimed specifically at staff working in pre-school education settings and the early years of primary and special schools. It seeks to develop the four capacities of children as successful learners, confident individuals, responsible citizens and effective contributors. It encourages a smoother transition from pre-school to Primary 1, with a focus on more directed teaching methods when the child is developmentally ready. The role of staff is discussed, as is the need for sensitive intervention and the importance of involving parents, but the Key Person approach is not mentioned.

Wales

The Foundation Phase is a framework of learning for children from the ages of three to seven. It replaced the previous *Desirable Outcomes for Children's Learning before Compulsory School Age* (ACAC, 2000) and the Programmes of Study in Key Stage 1 of the National Curriculum. It is issued under Sections 102, 105 and 108 of the Education Act 2002 by the Welsh Assembly Government.

Areas of Learning

There are seven statutory Areas of Learning in the Foundation Phase. For each Area of Learning there are educational programmes setting out what children should be taught, and the expected standards of children's performance. The seven Areas of Learning are:

- **Personal and Social Development, Well-Being and Cultural Diversity**

- **Language, Literacy and Communication Skills**

- **Mathematical Development**

- **Knowledge and Understanding of the World**

- **Bilingualism and Multicultural Understanding**

- **Creative Development**

- **Physical Development.**

The Foundation Phase links to the non-statutory *Skills Framework for 3 to 19 Year Olds in Wales* (Welsh Assembly Government, 2008b) which provides guidance on continuity and progression in developing thinking, communication, ICT and number for learners from three to nineteen. It also contributes to the Curriculum Cymreig, by developing children's understanding of the cultural identity unique to Wales in an integrated way across all seven Areas of Learning.

Emotional development

While the Key Person approach is not explicitly mentioned within the Foundation Phase framework, the importance of children's emotional development and well-being is recognised. The framework also strongly advocates positive links between the homes and the providers of care and education. In addition, it emphasises that:

'Practitioners must understand how children develop, and plan an appropriate curriculum that takes account of children's developmental needs and the skills they need to grow to become confident learners.' (Welsh Assembly Government, 2008a).

This indicates a personalised approach to the curriculum, where practitioners are knowledgeable about their individual children:

'Settings/schools should use material in ways suitable for children's age, experience, understanding and prior achievement to engage them in the learning process.' (Welsh Assembly Government, 2008a)

Personal and Social Development, Well-Being and Cultural Diversity are placed at the heart of the Foundation Phase. Developing relationships is naturally positioned as a skill within Social Development. The Well-being section states that children should be given the opportunity to understand their own feelings and the feelings of others, and be able to ask for assistance when it is needed. In moral and spiritual development, children need to be provided with activities that allow them to feel safe, secure and valued.

Similarly, in the *Observing Children* guidance (Welsh Assembly Government, 2008c) within Personal Development, suggested questions to consider when observing children's skills include:

'How do the children respond to being separated from their family? If they find it difficult, how long does it take for them to calm down and by what means are children comforted?'

Within Social Development there is a question on relationships and within Well-being and Cultural Diversity, there are questions on how children relate to others and are sufficiently confident to ask practitioners questions. These statements and questions contain many of the main aspects of the Key Person approach, but they are spread diffusely within the Foundation Phase curriculum rather than being brought together within a role explicitly labelled 'Key Person'.

In the *Learning and Teaching Pedagogy* guidance (Welsh Assembly Government, 2008d), the importance of children's interests is also raised as a way of promoting children's involvement in their learning (Laevers, 1994). This again indicates a personalised approach to the curriculum. The role of the practitioner in the Foundation Phase is that of a facilitator, where they have a good understanding of child development and individual children. This is reflected in the list of educational theorists and psychologists (although this does not include Bowlby), and areas of current research/learning theories, where emotional intelligence and well-being are cited among others.

Northern Ireland

The document *Curricular Guidance for Pre-School Education in Northern Ireland* provides guidance for those working with children in a range of pre-school settings, prior to primary schools and compulsory education in Northern Ireland. Settings are encouraged to use the guidance alongside other self-evaluation materials, such as *Together Towards Improvement: A Process for Self-Evaluation – Pre-school Education* (The Education and Training Inspectorate 2004). The guidance is intended for use in a range of settings and is used by staff to review, develop and promote good practice.

The Curricular Guidance describes what the pre-school child needs, and includes:

> 'interaction with sensitive and understanding adults who promote their sense of well-being and extend their learning and development, and adults who will treat them as individuals, support them and sensitively participate in their play.'

The guidance describes the need for staff to be knowledgeable about the ways in which children develop and learn, but stresses that the requirements and interests of individual children should come first in any work in the setting. It also encourages staff to give children time; to be responsive to children and to build partnerships with parents. This is not referred to as the Key Person approach, but contains many similar ideas.

Attachment and stability

The *Curricular Guidance* directs staff needing more information to *Birth to Three Matters* (Sure Start 2003). Within Birth to Three Matters: A Review of Literature (David et al, 2003), there is an emphasis placed on practitioners understanding:

> '...the importance of attachment and the importance of a child being special to at least one significant person to promote resilience.'

The *Birth to Three Matters* literature review adds:

> 'It is preferable to have stability in relationships with children and practitioners. A key worker system, with a small number of individually designated practitioners relating to particular children, as advised by Elfer et al (2002) enables responsiveness and sensitivity to individual children.'

This is tempered by the recognition that in other countries, such as Italy, children do not have a significant adult to interact with, but are encouraged to interact with a small, stable group of adults and children and with their environment. This emphasises the need for predictability and regularity in key relationships. The *Birth to Three Matters* literature review cites Selleck and Griffin (1996) to help practitioners to understand that they are not a replacement for parents, but instead form a special relationship that nourishes and protects. This relationship should be available regularly and predictably while the young child attends the setting. The importance of a practitioner's acceptance of a young child should not be dependent on the child's behaviour, but offered without judgement. Unconditional positive regard is emphasised.

Within the *Curricular Guidance*, the area of Personal, Social and Emotional Development is seen as being of utmost importance in children's lives. It highlights that practitioners need to build relationships with both the children and parents. Members of staff should be encouraged to work together, in order to enable children to feel secure and have a sense of well-being.

Key messages

Remember that:

- All curricula in the United Kingdom recognise the importance of well-being to children's development and learning, although they don't all refer explicitly to the term 'Key Person approach'.

- The Key Person approach is central to the EYFS in England (DfE 2012).

- The Key Person is discussed within the 'role of staff' feature of practice in the Scottish document *Pre-Birth to Three: Positive Outcomes for Scotland's Children and Families* (Learning and Teaching Scotland, 2010).

Chapter 3

What does the Key Person do?

This chapter examines what Goldschmied and Selleck (1996) describe as 'a triangle of trust and communication' between the parent or carer, the child and the key person. The diagram below shows the main stakeholders within the Key Person approach and how they relate to each other:

- **the child**

- **the parent** (this includes the significant adults in the child's life at home)

- **the Key Person**

- **the setting** (including other staff and the manager).

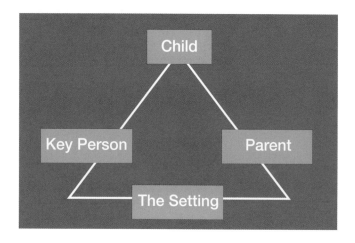

Main aspects of the Key Person role

The EYFS perspective on the Key Person is helpful in examining the main aspects of the role. The Key Person commitment (DfE 2008a cited on the Foundation Years website 2012) is:

> 'A key person has special responsibilities for working with a small number of children, giving them the reassurance to feel safe and cared for and building relationships with their parents.'

This emphasises that the role of a Key Person is to work with a number of children and their parents. While the exact number is not mentioned, the commitment does use the word 'small', showing that the Key Person should have a limited number of children and parents in order to work effectively.

The commitment also highlights the responsibilities of the Key Person as:

- **giving reassurance to their key children**

- **enabling their key children to feel safe**

- **supporting the care of their key children**

- **building relationships with their key children's parents.**

> 'Each child must be assigned a key person. Providers must inform parents and/or carers of the name of the key person, and explain their role, when a child starts attending a setting. The key person must help ensure that every child's learning and care is tailored to meet their individual needs. The key person must seek to engage and support parents and/or carers in guiding their child's development at home. They should also help families engage with more specialist support if appropriate. (page 7, DfE 2012)

The role of the key person in the EYFS (DfE 2012) adds an additional role for the key person in relation to the parents, encouraging the parents to support their child's development at home and also to access specialist support as needed. The role of the key person in relation to the child is not placed as central, although the key person holds an important role in ensuring individual care and learning needs are met. This has similarities to Scotland's approach.

Similarly, within *Pre-Birth to Three: Positive Outcomes for Scotland's Children and Families* (Learning and Teaching Scotland, 2010) the Key Person is included within the role of staff as an effective feature of practice. There is a lengthy description of the role of the Key Person as an anchor for their key children, to support planning for the individual child and to enable good communication with parents, the child's family and other agencies.

This links with Howes' (1999) research on the key determinants as to whether a child forms a bond with non-maternal caregivers (see Chapter 1, page 15 and Chapter 4, page 36). Where care is provided for children outside the family, there needs to be a consistent early years practitioner who is with the child regularly within their time at the setting to create a predictable pattern in interactions. This Key Person needs to provide physical and emotional care to the child, and to invest in the child at an emotional level.

In turn this relates to the *Early Years Learning and Development Review* (Evangelou et al, 2009) which identified the key aspects of relationships (outlined in Chapter 1, see page16).

The key worker role

Howes' research, the Early Years Learning and Development Review's work on relationships and the EYFS (DfE 2012) give a clear indication that the **Key Person** approach differs from the **key worker** role. While the terms 'key worker' and 'Key Person' can at times be used interchangeably in early years settings, Elfer, Goldschmied and Selleck (2003) emphasise that there is an important distinction to be made.

In social care and hospitals, the term key worker can be used and this tends to describe a role that is about liaison or co-ordinating between different professionals or between different disciplines, ensuring that services work in a co-ordinated way. Within the Early Support approach the role of the key worker is to maintain regular contact with the family, take responsibility for checking that all the necessary information is available, services are well-co-ordinated and that information about the child is shared efficiently with everyone who is working with the family.

Within early years settings the term key worker tends to mean that the practitioner has an administrative or paperwork focus to their work with the child, where the key worker works to ensure there is smooth transition and record keeping. However this key worker role is only a part of being a Key Person, which emphasises the emotional relationship above the organisational role.

Benefits of the Key Person approach

Elfer et al (2003) suggest that the Key Person approach has clear benefits for all four of the following key stakeholders:

For the child:

> I feel like I have someone I can rely on when I am at the setting.

> I feel special to someone when I am away from home.

> I feel I am cherished and known as an individual with my own special thoughts, interests and ideas by my Key Person.

Elfer et al (2003) explain how the child is helped to feel special and individual by their Key Person. The child feels that the Key Person thinks about them even when they are not there, in a similar way to how parents and carers respond to their children. This is demonstrated through comments such as:

'I thought about you while you were gone...'

'I wondered what you were doing today...'

For the parents:

The Key Person is not viewed by the parent as a competitor for the child's affection, but instead as a partner in the relationship with the child. It also allows a point of contact so the parent knows who to talk to, rather than being faced with a sea of different and unfamiliar faces.

> I know who to go and talk to when I go to the setting.

> I have peace of mind and can relax while my child is away from me at their setting.

> I can build a partnership with a Key Person in the setting and share with them the highs and the lows of bringing up my child.

> I can talk to someone who really knows my child well and is fully committed to them.

For the Key Person:

The Key Person faces strong emotional and physical demands from both the child and their parents/carers. However the Key Person also knows that they really matter to both the child and the parents/carers and they can gain satisfaction from the responsibility and impact they will have.

> I feel like I really matter to my key children and their families.

> I make a difference to my key children and how they feel at the setting.

> I know my key child very well and how to help them feel settled at the setting, and what helps them to learn and develop. This helps me in my role.

For the setting:

Elfer et al (2003) believe there are strong indications that settings which use the Key Person approach are more likely to have involved and satisfied staff, which in turn has an impact on turnover. The staff feel a responsibility and satisfaction about their work and are therefore likely to feel more engaged.

The Key Person approach helps all stakeholders, although it is not without its challenges and dilemmas. We look at these in Chapter 11.

> The staff feel more satisifed and engaged in working and playing with their children and families at the setting. This can reduce staff sickness and absence and develop involvement in professional development.

> The parents trust the staff more and are more confident of their abilites, qualities and care for their children.

> The care, learning and development for the children is much better because the staff know their key children more.

Key messages

- **The Key Person approach is important to and has benefits for the children, parents, practitioners and the setting.**

- **There is a difference between the Key Person approach and the key worker system.**

Chapter 4

Promoting shared care between the Key Person and home

This chapter looks at the ways in which shared care between home and the setting can be developed in order to strengthen the bond between the parent and the Key Person. The red arrow shows the aspect of the Key person approach that is being focused on.

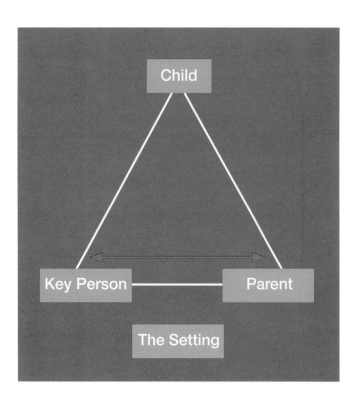

How does shared care relate to the EYFS (DCSF, 2008a)?

The Key Person Principle into Practice card in the EYFS (DCSF 2008a cited in Foundation Years 2012) states that shared care is one of the three most important aspects of the Key Person commitment:

> 'A key person has **special responsibilities** for working with a small number of children, giving them the reassurance to feel **safe** and cared for and building relationships with their parents.'

Within the section on shared care, the following key ideas are identified:

- **'A key person meets the needs of each child in their care and responds sensitively to their feelings, ideas and behaviour.**

- **A key person talks to parents to make sure that the child is being cared for appropriately for each family.**

- **A close emotional relationship with a key person in the setting does not undermine children's ties with their own parents.**

- **Careful records of the child's development and progress are created and shared by parents, the child, the key person and other professionals as necessary.'**

(Principles into Practice card 2.4: Key Person) (DCSF, 2008a)

These key ideas emphasise the importance of the relationships between the child, the Key Person and the parent/carer. It highlights the need for communication between the parent/carer and the Key Person on a regular basis and also the role that the Key Person holds in coordinating the child's learning and development records.

Why do children need shared care between home and the setting?

In the *Effective Practice* article on the Key Person in the EYFS (DfE 2008a) it states that when the Key Person approach is adopted, the Key Person is responsible for greeting their children, feeding their children and changing their children's nappies, which in turn creates a bond with their children.

The Key Person should be taking the lead role in caring for the child in the early years setting. It recognises that bonding is built up through the acts of caring for the child. It also highlights that care is not merely another part of the day, but should be valued by the Key Person as a way to get to know the child and be attuned to them.

In order to consider shared care, it is important to know when care occurs. This is difficult as care is something that a practitioner may do for a child all the time within a child's day. However there are times when caring is more apparent such as when a child:

- **is having their nappy changed or is being cleaned**

- **is eating and drinking**

- **is going to sleep**

- **needs comfort.**

These are key times of the day relating to care and are therefore important parts of a day for the child.

Howes (1999) states that the key determinants as to whether a child forms a bond with non-maternal caregivers include:

1. **whether the caregiver provides both physical and emotional care**

2. **whether that person is a consistent presence within the child's social network**

3. **whether the caregiver has an emotional investment in the child.**

When care is not provided by the members of the family, as within early years settings, Howes points out that there is a greater predictability in the pattern of interaction for the child when a caregiver is consistently present for longer periods of time. So it is important for early years practitioners to provide consistent physical and emotional care for their key children rather than this being shared out between all staff.

Selleck (2001) emphasises the importance of a continuing attachment relationship which link Key People who care for, play with and educate children in settings outside their homes in close association with children's significant attachment figures from home. Selleck argues that when babies are young:

> '...only the presence of a parent (or committed regular key person in the nursery) can provide the continuity, attention and sensuous pleasure the baby needs to make sense of all his or her experiences.'

Grenier (1999) terms the Key Person approach as:

> '...the commitment to providing consistent care and emotional support to each child, as an individual, throughout the day.'

He compares a thoughtful Key Person approach with that of impersonal nurseries. In impersonal nurseries the children's nappies are changed in a conveyor belt style by anyone or everyone as this is convenient to the setting. In comparison, in a thoughtful early years setting where the Key person approach is used, the child's nappy is changed by the Key Person who knows exactly how the child likes their nappy to be changed, the special rituals and routines that keep the child feeling happy and secure. In the impersonal nursery, nappy time is seen as routine and like a chore, and the opportunity for quality individual time with the key child is missed although it is recognised that there are other opportunities for quality time throughout the day. For the thoughtful setting, all staff work together and recognise the value of care routines as an opportunity for valuable individual time.

These authors all highlight the importance of the Key Person, where possible, taking responsibility for their key child's emotional and physical care. This means there has to be communication between setting and home about how care can and should be undertaken with the child.

How can shared care be created between setting and home?

There are a number of practical ways that shared care between home and setting can be encouraged to develop:

1 Gather information on how a child is cared for at home when they first join a setting.
The Key Person should find out about:

- **the nappy or toileting routine, including knowing how a child likes to be changed and the sequence the parent follows**

- **what and how a child likes to eat and drink**

- **when and how a child likes to go to sleep and wake from sleep**

- **how the child likes to be comforted.**

This information can be collected in a number of ways, through informal discussions on induction visits and through home visits.

2 Involve parents in the setting generally so they feel more able to share the details of their care routine with their child at home and build a bond with the Key Person.
This involvement of parents has to be carefully considered, to reflect the interests and needs of the parents.

Ideas to involve parents include:

- **events that are for adults alone such as social evenings**

- **asking parents to participate in the life of the setting through sharing their skills and talents**

- **parent workshops where the parent comes and plays in the setting with their child.**

3 Share information on how children have managed their day at drop off and pick up times.
This can be through having time to talk and chat or through having diary sheets/menu charts that inform parents when their child has eaten, had a drink, rested or had their nappy changed.

4 Provide accessible information sheets that show how children like to sleep, eat, drink and be comforted.
This can be in the form of fact sheets or passports for each child. These can be very useful for when staff changes occur. For children who may have complex health needs or disabilities, this is very important and may come in the form of a Family File (Early Support).

5 Review information on care routines and how a child likes to be cared for on a regular basis.
This is important to do regularly as children's preferences change at home and at the setting!

6 Ensure parents can make a time to speak to their Key Person if there is something they wish to talk about.
In busy settings, this may not be immediately but there needs to be flexibility to allow time for communication as soon as possible. It doesn't always need to be in person, sometimes an email or a telephone call will also allow that important communication to happen. It can be helpful to establish a parent's preferred means of communication at induction time and to review this on a regular basis.

7 Share the records of learning and development with parents on a regular basis.
It can be useful to remind parents they can look at the records whenever they choose. However it is also useful to have specific times throughout the year when the parents look at the record of learning and development with their Key Person and child. It is also important to encourage parents to contribute photographs and achievements that they have noticed their child do at home.

Key messages

- **A child needs a close warm relationship, a Key Person, to enable them to feel secure in each setting they attend.**

- **The Key Person needs to spend time building relationships with the parents of their key children.**

- **A Key Person needs to have a 'buddy' Key Person in settings other than childminders.**

How can I evaluate if there is shared care between the setting and home?

Here are a few questions to help you reflect on whether there is shared care:

∗   In your setting does each child have a named Key Person?

∗   How often does each Key Person have opportunities to talk to their key children's parents?

∗   Does this time include talking about how the family care for the child at home?

∗   How well does each Key Person recognise their key children's feelings?

∗   How well does each Key Person know their key children's interests and preferences?

∗   How well does each Key Person know how their key children are likely to behave and respond in different situations?

∗   How often are the child's learning and development records shared with the parents by the Key Person?

∗   How often do parents get an opportunity to contribute to these records?

∗   In terms of what Grenier calls a 'thoughtful' Key Person approach, where would each member of staff place the setting on the scale below?

| 1 | 2 | 3 | 4 | 5 | 6 | 7 | 8 | 9 | 10 |

Impersonal setting where care is done for convenience of setting and staff

Thoughtful setting where care is done for convenience of child

There are no correct answers to these questions, as all settings are different. However hopefully they will allow you to reflect on your practice in relation to shared care, celebrate what is being done well and decide on what needs further development.

The Key Person Approach © Anita Soni and Sue Bristow 2012

Chapter 5

Promoting a secure attachment between the Key Person and child

This chapter considers ways that a secure attachment between the Key Person and the child can be developed in order to strengthen this bond. The red arrow shows the aspect of the Key Person approach that is being focused on.

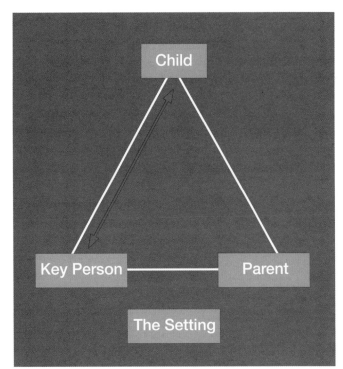

How does secure attachment relate to the EYFS (DCSF, 2008a)?

The Key Person Principle into Practice card in the EYFS (DCSF 2008a cited in Foundation Years 2012) states that secure attachment is one of the three most important aspects of the Key Person commitment:

> 'A key person has **special responsibilities** for working with a small number of children, giving them the reassurance to feel **safe** and cared for and building relationships with their parents.'

Within the section on secure attachment, the following is identified:

- **'A key person helps the baby or child to become familiar with the setting and to feel confident and safe within it.**

- **A key person develops a genuine bond with children and offers a settled, close relationship.**

- **When children feel happy and secure in this way they are confident to explore and to try out new things.**

- **Even when children are older and can hold special people in mind for longer there is still a need for them to have a key person to depend on in the setting, such as their teacher or a teaching assistant.'**

(Principles into Practice card 2.4: Key Person DCSF 2008a)

These ideas emphasise the importance of the relationships between the child and the Key Person. The Key Person's role is crucial in transition and in helping the child to feel comfortable and confident in the setting. The importance of having a Key Person right through the EYFS is stressed, for young babies through to five-year-olds in Reception classes.

Why do children need a secure attachment in their setting?

The PSED training materials (Sure Start, 2006) explain that humans as babies have an inbuilt desire to form a close emotional tie with their closest caregiver. This attachment is vital as it ensures the survival, care and nurturing of the baby and therefore gives the baby a sense of security.

This early close relationship is influential as it affects many aspects of children's development, including their language, behaviour and relationships with others. The nature of these early bonds becomes the blueprint for the comfort, care and closeness that babies and young children expect from other relationships throughout childhood and into later life.

Once a baby or child starts to go to a setting beyond their home, they need to build a close relationship there to allow them to feel safe, settled and confident to learn and develop. This bond with a Key Person in the setting does not undermine the child's attachment with their parent, as a child is able to have a small number of close bonds (just as each child is likely to have within their family). Selleck and Griffin (1996) explain that an early years practitioner builds an additional separate relationship with the child as s/he:

> '...must also develop a strong and complementary attachment to the infants and toddlers in her care. She will not be a substitute for mothers or fathers or grannies, but she must be able to form a special relationship which can nourish and protect, and is available on a regular and predictable basis during the day.'

The Key Person is not replacing the parent, but is instead developing a new special relationship that the child can rely on.

Roberts (2002) emphasises the importance of the practitioners being able to accept all aspects of a child without judgement, what is sometimes termed 'unconditional positive regard':

> 'the sort of acceptance that babies and young children need from parents and other important people is not acceptance that is dependent on their behaviour; it is acceptance without reservations and without judgements. It can be described as 'unconditional positive regard' ...Babies learn that they are acceptable by experiencing, day by day, the results of that acceptance ...when an 'important person' smiles at the baby, and when that person comes at the baby's call, the sense that he or she is acceptable is confirmed. This is not simply a passive process; all the time the baby is learning by experience how to win the smiles, how to bring the person. Every experience is a learning experience.'

In the *Birth to Three Matters* review of literature, David et al (2003) highlight key messages that can be learnt from attachment research:

- **It is preferable to have stability in relationships with children and practitioners.**

- **A key worker system, with a small number of individually designated practitioners relating to particular children, as advised by Elfer et al (2003) enables responsiveness and sensitivity to individual children.**

So, in addition to advocating complementary attachments with practitioners, which ensure responsive and loving attention (Goldschmied and Jackson 1994), Selleck and Griffin (1996) agree with Roberts (2002) that effective practice between birth and three will provide individual children with opportunities to develop a positive self-concept, interdependent relationships and a personal identity.

A recurring theme from the review of Personal, Social and Emotional literature for the EYFS (Evangelou et al, 2009) is the importance of warmth and security in a child's principal relationships to a child's development and learning. This is viewed as the foundation upon which a child can build their learning and development. A second key theme is the need for the adult to be warm, responsive and contingent to the needs of the child. This implies that adults need to be carefully attuned to their key children and be ready to adjust their response according to the changing needs of the child.

The PSED training materials (Sure Start, 2006) explain there are three building blocks that enable children and practitioners to have a close bond: feeling secure; separating and exploring; and seeking help and comfort when needed. These are discussed in greater depth in Chapter 1, and can help you understand how a secure attachment influences the way in which babies and young children explore and learn about the world and how they feel and see themselves and others. The implication of the three building blocks is that the Key Person needs to be able to develop a genuine bond with a child in order to offer a settled, close relationship in which they can provide warm, sensitive care readily and willingly so that all children can seek comfort and support when they need it.

How can a secure attachment between the Key Person and child be promoted in the setting?

1 When a child first starts at a setting, it is important that the Key Person gathers information from parents and the family on what the child likes and doesn't like. This includes knowing:

- **what the child likes to play with**

- **what the child doesn't like or is wary of**

- **what the child may find difficult**

- **what stories and songs the child is familiar with**

- **who the child may know at the setting**

- **how the child may respond to new situations**

- **what comforts or soothes the child.**

This information can be gathered in a number of ways, through informal discussions on induction visits and through home visits. Consider how these views are gathered, as parents, just like children, can be quick to give the 'correct' answers that they think are the ones the practitioner wants to hear!

2 Involve parents in the setting generally so they feel more able to share the details of what their child has been doing at home and build a bond with the Key Person. This involvement of parents has to be carefully considered, to reflect the particular interests and needs of the parents at your setting. You could try:

- **diary sheets that ask for information on what the child has done at home**

- **informal chats when the child arrives or leaves**

- **asking parents to bring leaflets of places they have visited**

- **news time where children talk about what they have done**

- **asking children to bring in toys or items from home**

- **providing a teddy bear who goes home with children, finding out what they like to play with, read, watch on television or places they visit.**

3 Share information on what children have enjoyed and played with during their time at the setting. This can be done through photograph displays of the day's or week's events. It can also be useful to have a digital photograph frame. In some settings, having a special message book for parents to show what their child loved that day can be a quick way of sharing information. Alternatively have a sticker that says 'I enjoyed doing …'. This reassures the parent about leaving their child in the setting, which in turn helps the child feel more settled and secure.

4 Have a photograph display showing parents, staff and children who the Key Person is and their key children. This display can be enhanced with children's drawings and comments, showing what the children like about their Key Person, or explaining what each child likes to do and play with. This will help the child see their Key Person as special, rather than them simply being in the blue or the red group.

5 Each Key Person needs to spend time on a regular basis with each of their key children, individually or within a group. This needs to go beyond having time to comfort and settle children, but also needs to build in enjoyable happy time together. With the youngest children this can be done through ensuring the Key Person does the care routine of feeding or changing a nappy, as these can be special, enjoyable times too!

6 The planning should reflect children's interests and each Key Person needs to input into the planning process to ensure that there are activities and experiences that reflect each of their key children's interests and needs.

7 Each Key Person needs to take an active interest in each of their key children's lives, so they can comment, ask questions and show that they think about their children. With the youngest children, this can be through talking to the parents and carers but also spending time with the child themselves talking and listening.

8 Any information on interests and what a child likes to do and play with will need reviewing on a regular basis. This is important to do, as children's preferences can change quickly both at home and at the setting!

9 It is important that if a child wants comfort or support, they know they can have time to be with and/or speak to their Key Person. In busy settings with older children, this may not always be immediately but there needs to be flexibility to allow time as soon as possible. It can be useful if there are ways children can indicate a need for a chat or time together. In some settings this may be leaving a peg next to their name, or knowing when the staff are available and free to talk.

10 The records of learning and development need to be shared with the children on a regular basis, based on their age and stage of development. This can extend to children selecting the work and photographs that go into the book and helping to compile it. It is useful to have regular times throughout the year when the children can look at the record of learning and development with their Key Person and can add comments. It is also important to encourage children and parents to contribute photographs and achievements that they have done outside the setting. This is a lovely opportunity to review progress with the child and see how they have learnt, developed and grown.

Key messages

- An attachment is shown when babies and young children seek warm, close relationships with their parents and other primary caregivers such as their Key Person.

- Building a secure attachment is made up of three building blocks: feeling secure, separating and exploring, and seeking help and comfort when needed.

- The importance of a secure attachment has been linked to promoting a child's social and emotional development.

- High quality settings are signified by warm, responsive relationships between adults and children that recognise the individuality of the child.

- Babies and young children can have a few close relationships and the relationship with the Key Person does not affect other close relationships with the family.

- A child needs a close warm relationship, a Key Person, to enable them to feel secure in each setting they attend.

- A child's need for the Key Person approach does not end at a certain age but continues throughout their early years.

How can I evaluate if the children have a secure attachment to their Key Person in the setting?

Here are a few questions to help you reflect on whether there is a secure attachment for each child in the setting:

* In your setting does each child have a named Key Person?

* Can each Key Person write a list of their key children in their group? Once they have written them all down, it can be useful to reflect upon who was last to come into the practitioner's mind and why?

* For each Key Person's list of key children, can they write three special things that they know about each child, such as their favourite toy, what they dislike eating, and the names of any pets, siblings and so on?

* Does each Key Person in the setting know who they are a 'buddy' Key Person for?

* Does each Key Person know how each key child likes to be comforted when upset or distressed?

* Does each Key Person know where and when a key child is likely to get anxious or worried?

* Think back over the previous week. When did each Key Person spend a little time playing and talking with each key child? This can include feeding and changing times.

* How often does each Key Person welcome their key child into the setting or get to say goodbye?

* Does each Key Person do the induction visits or home visits with the new child?

* When do the Key People have an opportunity to talk about the children and how they feel about them?

* Ask each of the children who is their Key Person or who would they go to for a hug if they were hurt?

* When does the Key Person have an opportunity to share the child's learning journey with them? This needs to reflect the child's age and stage of development and interest in doing so.

* Where would each Key Person place the setting on the scale below?

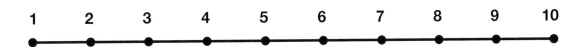

| 1 | 2 | 3 | 4 | 5 | 6 | 7 | 8 | 9 | 10 |

Impersonal setting where care is done for convenience of setting and staff

Thoughtful setting where care is done for convenience of child

There are no correct answers to these questions, as all settings are different. However hopefully they will allow you to reflect on your practice in relation to shared care, celebrate what is being done well and decide on what needs further development.

Chapter 6

Promoting the independence of the children

This chapter considers ways that children's independence can be promoted while maintaining a Key person approach. The red arrow shows the link between the setting and the child. The child is seeking to develop independence while maintaining a secure attachment with their Key Person and their parents.

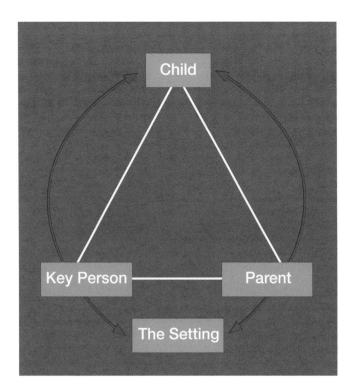

How does independence relate to the EYFS?

(DCSF 2008a as cited on Foundation Years website 2012)

The EYFS (DCSF 2008a) states that secure attachment is one of the three most important aspects of the Key Person commitment:

> 'A key person has special responsibilities for working with a small number of children, giving them the reassurance to feel safe and cared for and building relationships with their parents.'

Within the section on independence, the following is identified:

- **'Babies and children become independent by being able to depend upon adults for reassurance and comfort.**

- **Children's independence is most obvious when they feel confident and self-assured, such as when they are in their own home with family, or with friends and familiar carers such as a key person.**

- **Babies and children are likely to be much less independent when they are in new situations, such as a new group or when they feel unwell or anxious.'**

(Principles into Practice card 2.4: Key Person DCSF 2008a)

So the relationship between the child and the Key Person is very important in building a child's independence. It stresses the Key Person's role in helping the child to feel comfortable and confident in the setting so that the child can then feel able to explore independently and securely, knowing that they have their Key Person to fall back on when they need to.

Why do children need to build up their independence in the setting?

The PSED materials (Sure Start 2006) identify three building blocks for children to make a close emotional attachment with their Key Person as feeling secure; separating and exploring; and seeking help and comfort when needed (See Chapter 1, page 8 and Chapter 5, page 43).

These building blocks remind us that in order to develop independence, children first have to know they can be dependent upon someone, their Key Person in the setting. It may feel counter-intuitive to staff that they have to let children build a relationship before they feel able to go and explore in an independent way. Indeed it is recognised as a potential obstacle to the Key Person approach (DCSF, 2008a) that staff may feel the child is likely to become too dependent on the Key Person. This is discussed further in Chapter 11.

Goldschmied and Jackson (1994) remind us that children aged between one and two get the least planned attention by staff and are also considered to be the most challenging. This reflects the developmental stage of the child, where they are keen to assert their own mind and independence about the many things that interest them, but simultaneously still need high levels of comfort and help as soon as it is needed. Goldschmied and Jackson tell us:

> '...that independence, though exciting and desired, can also be rather frightening. We need a secure base in order to have the confidence to venture out from it.'

David et al (2003) in the *Birth to Three Matters* Review of Literature highlight how the transition from babyhood to early childhood is a time when the child has a growing sense of self. Dunn (1993) states that children are becoming aware of how others view them and this in turn has an impact on the child's self-competence and self-worth. At the same time as this growing sense of how others view them, the child is also developing a sense of independence (Karmiloff-Smith 1994). Therefore if a child is told through body language and words that they are capable and competent when attempting to be independent, this will promote their self-esteem and positive view of themselves.

Roberts (2002) reminds practitioners that in order to raise children's self-esteem, they should create situations where children are able to succeed in the tasks they set for themselves or if not, at least be able to express how frustrated they feel to someone who will care and understand – their Key Person!

How well the Key Person knows a child is essential to providing the right level of autonomy for the child to develop as an independent learner.

A dictionary definition of autonomous cited by Featherstone and Bayley (2001) is:

> '...acting independently or having the freedom to do so.'

The skill of the practitioner is to offer the child the room to grow within safe but challenging boundaries where a child can explore without fear of failure.

It is important also that the Key Person appreciates that a child's ability to be independent can be different with different people and situations. Take, for example, when a child moves rooms or falls and bumps their knee. In both situations they will need to 'seek comfort and help' before they can again feel confident to explore. Our need for a Key Person at times of 'crisis' can continue beyond our early years and into adulthood!

> 'What a child can do with assistance today she will be able to do herself tomorrow.'
> (Vygotsky, 1962)

Key messages

- **Building a secure attachment is made up of three building blocks: feeling secure, separating and exploring, and seeking help and comfort when needed.**

- **The setting's environment has to provide opportunities for a child to be independent.**

- **The Key Person promotes independence by both being a secure base for their key children and providing freedom to explore and learn.**

How can independence for the child be promoted in the setting?

Independence is often considered in terms of the physical learning environment both inside and outside. It is important also to consider the emotional environment. The following questionnaire aims to reflect both aspects of the environment and should be completed from the child's perspective:

Independence audit from the child's perspective

Imagine you are a child in your setting or room, and try to answer the questions below:

Access

∗ Can I choose what I want to play with in the way I want to? For most of the day?

∗ Can I choose from a range of resources during adult-led activities?

∗ Do I know how many of my friends can play in the sand and the water? Can I get drink and food as I need it?

∗ Can I sleep when I am tired?

∗ Can I go outside as often as I want to?

Organisation

∗ Can I find the things I need or want to play with?

∗ Can I tidy up without adult help? How do I know where things go?

∗ When I move rooms can I still find my chosen things?

∗ Have I got a space for my things, such as my comforter, drawings?

∗ Am I involved in planning and developing my environment?

∗ Can I display my work?

∗ Do the adults observe me using the learning environment and make changes to improve it as a result?

Location

∗ Do I have to go a long way for the toys I need?

∗ Are the resources I need for my play located nearby?

∗ Can I carry the toys I choose to play with?

∗ Can I get to my things/my bag?

Quality and presentation

∗ Do I want to play with the toys I see at the setting?

∗ Are the toys checked for missing pieces?

∗ Are there new things available to play with?

∗ Do the resources look engaging?

∗ Can I see what is on offer to play with or eat or drink?

Sufficiency

∗ Are there enough of each type of toy for me and my friends to play with?

∗ e.g. Are there enough bikes?

∗ e.g. Are there enough construction wheels or play people?

The Key Person Approach © Anita Soni and Sue Bristow 2012

Suitability

* Do the toys do what I want them to do and are meant to do?

* Do the scissors cut?

* Are the pencils sharp and do the felt-tipped pens work?

* Does the play furniture fit the dolls' house?

* Are the jigsaw puzzles too easy or too hard?

* Is the construction too small/large for my fingers?

* Are the balls and outdoor equipment the right size for me?

Routines

* Can I go outside when I choose to?

* Do the adults follow my routine so if I choose to play with my toys for longer I can or if I feel tired can I go and have a rest?

* Can I have a drink or eat if I need to?

* Am I encouraged to put my coat on/get dressed myself at my own pace?

* How am I encouraged to accept the choice of food and drink that is offered?

* How do adults encourage me to make independent choices and accept when those choices may conflict with the adult's views?

Range

* Do I see my family and the community where I live in the toys I play with?

* Do the resources available reflect my interests and learning needs?

* Do I have opportunities to try new experiences inside and outside?

Adults and other children

* Do I have a Key Person who takes a special interest in me?

* Do the adults help me play and learn by playing alongside me?

* Am I allowed to make mistakes and take risks?

* Do the adults help me to be autonomous in my learning and to make choices?

* Can I play in pairs, small groups and larger groups when I choose to?

* Am I encouraged to play independently; to explore what I can do with less dependence on adults?

* Can I get comfort and help when I need it?

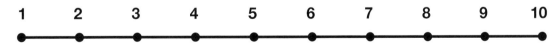

| 1 | 2 | 3 | 4 | 5 | 6 | 7 | 8 | 9 | 10 |

No independence
for children

Children are fully
independent

There are no correct answers to these questions, as all settings are different. However hopefully they will allow you to reflect on your practice in relation to shared care, celebrate what is being done well and decide on what needs further development.

Chapter 7

Observation, assessment and planning

This chapter examines the role of the Key Person in relation to observation, assessment and planning. It considers the different roles practitioners may perform within each day, and how these should be prioritised within the Key Person approach. It goes on to suggest the unique way in which the Key Person role can be used to support observation, assessment and planning.

The Key Person as a practitioner

As we have discussed, the Key Person approach emphasises the need for young children and babies to build a close bond with their Key Person. However in practice this emphasis can be easily replaced as other aspects of the practitioner role demand attention.

There are many different elements to the role of early years practitioner. Just take a moment to think how many tasks you undertake within a day. There may be domestic duties relating to food or drink preparation and keeping areas of the room tidy and clean. There may be practical and organisational issues such as ensuring toys are easily available, the room is well organised and that necessary items are to hand. There may also be administrative and paperwork tasks such as writing observations, checking risk assessments and writing plans.

Think about the many 'hats' a practitioner might wear during a day. These may include:

- **the organiser with her clipboard, supervising and overseeing the children**

- **the cook and cleaner with the domestic roles of preparing and serving food and drink and keeping the space tidy**

- **the secretary who does the writing and record-keeping**

- **the carer who comforts and supports their key children when they need it**

- **the liaison officer who listens and talks to parents/carers about their child and any concerns or positive moments they wish to share.**

The Key Person role contains aspects of all of the above and others you may have thought of, but the priority is given to the caring role of building relationships with the key children and their parents.

Grenier (1999) says the Key Person approach can be considered in two ways, firstly:

> 'The key person approach is generally taken to mean that a small group of children is assigned to be overseen by a particular adult – with that adult compiling observations and reports, and liaising with the parents.'

This does seem to be a common understanding of the Key Person approach, reflecting a prioritisation of the organiser role or liaison officer role. However Grenier goes on to add:

> 'This is a very inadequate understanding of the approach, which should be fundamentally about the commitment to providing consistent care and emotional support to each child, as an individual, throughout the day.'

The emotional and relationship aspect of the Key Person approach is also highlighted by Elfer, Goldschmied and Selleck (2003), within the *EYFS (DfE 2012)* and *Pre-Birth to Three (Learning and Teaching* Scotland, 2010).

The Key Person approach and the key worker role

We have looked closely at the differences between the Key Person and key worker roles in Chapter 3 (see page 31). Within early years settings the term key worker tends to mean the practitioner has an administrative or paperwork focus to their work with their key children, where the key worker ensures there is smooth transition and record-keeping. However this key worker role is only a part of being a Key Person, which emphasises the emotional relationship rather than the organisational role. The Key Person role has the key worker role as part of the duties, but the emphasis is on the building of strong relationships with the key child and their parents and carers.

The Key Person's role in observation, assessment and record keeping

One of the most frequently asked questions by practitioners is: Should the Key Person be doing all of the observations of their key children?

The two concepts of observation and recording need to be separated out, as all the staff at the setting, and the parents and indeed the other children all observe and notice different things about the key child. Therefore the question may not be who observes the key child, as clearly everyone does. The question may more appropriately be: Should the Key Person be recording all the observations of their key children?

This should be considered from a number of viewpoints:

- **From the Key Person's perspective, this is ineffective as it can mean that important moments are not observed if the child's Key Person is unavailable (they may be at lunch, off that day or simply focused on something else in the setting).**

- **From the child's point of view, it may mean special moments are not observed if the Key Person is busy or unavailable and that they can only have moments worthy of recording if the Key Person is there. It may also be that only certain moments or activities are likely to be recorded as this is dependent upon the Key Person's perspective.**

- **From the parents' and carers' perspectives, this would indicate that the Key Person is the only person who can observe and record their child, and therefore other special moments may be missed including the ones at home that the parent sees!**

- **From the setting's perspective this can be seen as less effective and efficient as there is a reliance upon a Key Person recording all their observations despite attendance patterns of children and staff and the confidence of the staff.**

It is clear that everyone should be able to do observations of the children as this allows special moments to be captured as and when they occur. The need for multiple perspectives on the child is discussed within Creating the Picture (DfES 2007) and within the Development Matters for the EYFS (Early Education 2012);

'Observe children as they act and interact in their play, everyday activities and planned activities, and learn from parents about what their child does at home.' (p.3, Early Education, 2012)

While it is useful for everyone involved to observe the child, the Key Person's role is to collate the observations, and discuss them with the parents and the child. Indeed the building of the Learning Journey from the formative assessments (observations, photographs and samples of the child's work and play) can be a part of the quality time that the key person spends with the child, dependent on the child's stage of development. This in turn supports the Key Person to create a detailed, accurate and well rounded summative assessment (short summary of the child's development) which could be the EYFS progress check at two (NCB, 2012) or as an annual report to share with parents, or as the child leaves the room or setting.

The Key Person's role in planning

Another frequently asked question by practitioners is: Should the Key Person be planning all the activities and experiences for their key children?

Again this can be considered from a number of perspectives:

- **From the Key Person's perspective, this is ineffective and creates pressure as it means that the child can only access the activities organised by the Key Person and that they have to provide all the variety and opportunities themselves.**

- **From the child's point of view, it may mean that they can only access what the Key Person has planned, whereas there may be many things within the environment that excite and interest them.**

- **From the parents' and carers' perspective, this would indicate that the Key Person is the only person who can plan for their child, and therefore other opportunities may be missed!**

- **A stimulating learning environment, which offers high quality continuous provision is seen as key to supporting children's learning and development (Foundation Years website, 2012). This can be a good way of incorporating a wide range of children's different interests and needs.**

A more effective approach is for the Key Person to ensure their key children's 'voices' are heard somewhere in the planning for sessions and the environment. This may mean that:

- **Ideas are contributed by all the different Key People in a shared environment such as a room in a daycare setting, a nursery class or a playgroup. This can be done through a mechanism such as an ideas board where everyone can write ideas for the following day or week linked to their child, then the range of ideas can be incorporated into the planning.**

- **The Key People in a shared environment meet together to record the planning and share ideas, while bearing in mind their key children in their group and what they would enjoy and/ or need to experience the following week.**

- **The Key People in a shared environment review their previous day or week, and ask the children what experiences they would like the following week. This can be recorded in a simple way as planning. This can be by younger children placing smiley faces on the resources they have enjoyed, or reviewing photographs of the activities and experiences they have had that day or week.**

- **Continuous provision (activities and experiences that children access independently on a regular basis) are useful to fully incorporate the wide range of different key children's interests and needs.**

Key messages

- **A child needs a close warm relationship, a Key Person, to enable them to feel secure in each setting they attend.**

- **There is a difference between the Key Person approach and the key worker system.**

- **All practitioners in a setting and the parents and family can undertake observations of a child.**

- **Compiling a child's record may be a useful task for the Key Person to do with their key child as part of quality time together.**

- **The Key Person may not record and deliver all the planned activities for their key children, but instead can play a role in ensuring that their children's needs and interests are reflected in the planning.**

How can I evaluate the role of the Key Person within observation, assessment and planning?

Here are a few key questions to help you reflect on the role of the Key Person:

∗ In your setting does each child have a named Key Person?

∗ What do the practitioners see as the main aspects of their role as a Key Person?

∗ Do the practitioners understand the difference between a Key Person and a key worker?

∗ What role do the practitioners feel the Key Person has within observation of their key children?

∗ What role do the practitioners feel the Key Person has within planning for their key children?

∗ What role do the practitioners feel the Key Person has within record keeping for their key children?

∗ In terms of the basis of the Key Person approach, where would each member of staff place the setting on the following scale?

| 1 | 2 | 3 | 4 | 5 | 6 | 7 | 8 | 9 | 10 |

Paperwork-focused
Key Person approach

Relationship focused
Key Person approach

There are no correct answers to these questions, as all settings are different. However hopefully they will allow you to reflect on your practice in relation to shared care, celebrate what is being done well and decide on what needs further development.

The Key Person Approach © Anita Soni and Sue Bristow 2012

Chapter 8

Safeguarding children

This chapter explores ways of developing the Key Person approach while safeguarding and promoting the welfare of the children at all times.

What is safeguarding?

Working Together to Safeguard Children (DCSF, 2010) has defined the term 'safeguarding children' as:

> 'The process of protecting children from abuse or neglect, preventing impairment of their health and development, and ensuring they are growing up in circumstances consistent with the provision of safe and effective care that enables children to have optimum life chances and enter adulthood successfully.'

The concept of safeguarding has relevance to the Key Person approach as this is closely linked to providing children with a safe base, shared care and supporting independence. The Key Person's relationship is central to ensuring that the welfare of each child is closely monitored and any changes that cause concern, such as changes in behaviour, unexplained marks or a child's comment is reported in accordance with the setting's safeguarding policy.

The strength of the relationship between the Key Person and parents is crucial to understanding whether the observations that cause concern will need to be reported on or not. There may be a simple explanation for the concerns, for example, the parent has already informed the Key Person that the bruise on their child's head is from a fall on the way to nursery. In addition it is possible that parents may have developed sufficient trust to ensure any concerns about the welfare of their child they have are shared with their child's Key Person so that the relevant help can be sought.

In accordance with the Childcare Act 2006, providers have to adhere to the safeguarding and welfare requirements. The safeguarding and welfare requirements in the Statutory Framework for the EYFS (DfE 2012) are designed to help providers create high quality settings which are welcoming, safe and stimulating. Providers must take all necessary steps to keep children safe and well. There is specific guidance in relation to child protection:

> '3.6 Providers must train all their staff to understand their safeguarding policy and procedures, and ensure that all staff have up to date knowledge of safeguarding issues.'

Under suitable people it is stated:

> '3.9 Providers must ensure that people looking after children are suitable to fulfil the requirements of their roles.'

Staff:child ratios

> '3.27 Staffing arrangements must meet the needs of all children and ensure their safety. Providers must ensure that children are adequately supervised and decide how to deploy staff to ensure children's needs are being met.'

Information and records

> '3.67 Providers must maintain records and obtain and share information (with parents and carers, other professionals working with the child, and the police, social services and OfSTED as appropriate) to ensure the safe and efficient management of the setting, and to help ensure the needs of all children are met. Providers must enable a regular, two way flow of information with parents and/or carers, and between providers.'

These requirements do not directly mention the key person approach but have implications for it in settings.

Physical contact

For a Key Person to work effectively, they need to be able to respond as a parent would do to their child, while simultaneously maintaining a professional relationship that does not exceed boundaries. This balance of a professional yet close and warm relationship can be very difficult to achieve and a Key Person can be fearful of groundless allegations being made against them. This is particularly relevant with children who do need high levels of physical closeness in order to feel secure within the setting environment.

Responses from settings vary and can include:

- **to always put a cushion between themselves and the child if the child requires physical reassurance on a practitioner's lap**

- **discouraging children from sitting on their laps and removing children quite quickly if a child tries to initiate it.**

This type of reaction, while understandable, is likely to hinder the attachment process between Key Person and key child. For some children the type of relationship they are used to from home is very different to this approach. It can also be unsettling for very young babies whose need for physical closeness is vital. Indeed, denying a child the physical closeness within the setting could be viewed as a form of neglect. As Elfer et al. (2003) state:

> 'Denying children physical comforting and holding would be as abusive to youngsters as imposing it for adults' gratification.'

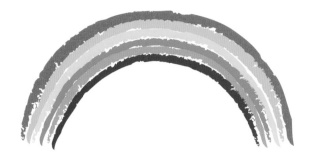

How can you be an effective Key Person and safeguard the children in your care?

We highly recommend that you take a common sense approach:

- **The setting discuss and agree, within the whole staff team, how to physically hold children and respond when children express their need for physical affection and/or physical contact, so an appropriate response is given, for example, cuddling a child to praise their good behaviour.**

- **Practitioners are made aware of the need to report and the procedure to follow if they have any concerns about a member of staff.**

- **Practitioners are never left alone with children.**

- **Clear guidelines are given to practitioners about outside contact with families who attend the setting such as through babysitting or social networking sites.**

- **Regular supervision is in place to ensure practitioners can talk to their manager or room senior or peers about incidences that have given them cause for concern in relation to themselves and other practitioners in the setting. (There is further discussion on support for the Key Person and supervision in Chapter 10.)**

- **The safeguarding policy is shared with parents on induction and throughout their time at the setting so that parents are aware of how the setting maintains a close, warm but also professional relationship with each child and family.**

- **There is regular training and updates on safeguarding, especially for practitioners who work with vulnerable families.**

There are a growing number of men working in the early year sector and it can be very difficult for them, as parents may have reservations about their child having their care needs such as nappy changing and feeding being met by a male carer. However, if the same common sense approaches are applied within the setting the benefits of having more men in childcare can still be enjoyed:

'parents have at various times expressed misgivings about men giving intimate care (nappy changing, toileting children etc.) ...These objections have been met by establishing and publicising a witnessing policy, whereby workers do not give intimate care alone but work together, and by pointing out to parents that if gender equality is achieved it will be because each gender is willing to give up its area of sole control.'
(Bateman 1998 from Elfer 2003)

The majority of parents will be reassured by this stance. However there may be instances linked to cultural, religious or other reasons where a compromise has to be openly discussed and agreed by all parties involved and reviewed periodically.

Lessons to be learnt

A number of high profile cases have heightened awareness of the dangers of physical and sexual abuse happening within early years settings. However while these cases can be upsetting or challenging to think about, there are a number of lessons to be learnt that are strengthening the infrastructure of the Key Person approach and safeguarding procedures within settings. *The Serious Case Review Overview Report* (Plymouth Safeguarding Children's Board March 2010) lists a number of recommendations for practitioners working in settings:

- **operate safer recruitment procedures, including value-based interviewing**

- **have effective policies and procedures in place which are communicated to staff, including child protection and intimate care**

- **encourage open discussions amongst the staff group about good and poor practice and facilitate constructive challenge of each other**

- **ensure that safeguarding is openly discussed and staff are aware of the possibility that abuse might happen within their workplace**

- **have effective whistle-blowing procedures**

- **have safeguards in place where boundaries may be blurred through friendship networks amongst staff and parents**

- **encourage communication and contact with parents and ensure they are kept well informed about their child's day to day experiences.**

Key messages

- **Your Key Person policy and Safeguarding policy must be linked.**

- **A child needs a close warm relationship, a Key Person, to enable them to feel secure in each setting they attend.**

- **The Key Person needs to spend time building relationships with the parents of their key children.**

- **The Key Person needs to spend time building relationships with their key children.**

- **A Key Person needs to have a 'back-up' Key Person in settings other than childminders.**

- **An effective Key Person is part of a wider team and needs to access regular supervision and support from the senior staff or manager.**

Safeguarding children audit

Here are a few key questions to help you reflect on your safeguarding children policy.

* In your setting does each child have a named Key Person?

* Does your induction process include an opportunity to discuss your specific Key Person approach in relation to the safeguarding policy?

* Is the effectiveness of your setting's relationship with parents closely monitored and individual families discussed?

* Does each Key Person in the setting have regular supervision where their relationship with each individual child and family is reviewed?

* Do you have effective whistle blowing procedures, and does this include what to do if there are concerns about the Designated Safeguarding Person (DSP)?

* Are staff recording observations of a child's behaviour and well-being especially when changes have been noticed? Are these observations being shared with the designated person responsible for safeguarding when the changes are noticed?

| 1 | 2 | 3 | 4 | 5 | 6 | 7 | 8 | 9 | 10 |

The Key Person Policy should link with the Safeguarding policy of the setting

Clear safeguarding policy that is cross-referenced with Key Person approach

There are no correct answers to these questions, as all settings are different. However hopefully they will allow you to reflect on your practice in relation to shared care, celebrate what is being done well and decide on what needs further development.

The Key Person Approach © Anita Soni and Sue Bristow 2012

Thinking critically

This chapter examines thinking critically, considering how it relates to sustained shared thinking, how it can be done and who is best placed to support children with this key skill.

What is critical thinking?

Thinking skills are usually divided into six main areas:

- **enquiry skills – asking questions and enquiring**

- **information-processing skills – linking different bits of information acquired**

- **reasoning skills – forming an opinion or an idea based on what has been seen**

- **evaluation skills – agreeing and disagreeing with ideas and making own judgements**

- **problem solving – trying a range of strategies to solve a problem**

- **creative-thinking skills – looking for new ways to try something out.**

These six aspects of thinking skills provide the background to sustained shared thinking. The EPPE (Effective Provisions of Pre-School) research (Sylva et al, 2004) identified a number of factors which contributed to a highly effective setting. One of these factors was sustained shared thinking which is defined as:

> '"Sustained shared thinking" occurs when two or more individuals 'work together' in an intellectual way to solve a problem, clarify a concept, evaluate an activity, extend a narrative etc. Both parties must contribute to the thinking and it must develop and extend the understanding. It was more likely to occur when the children were interacting 1:1 with an adult or with a single peer partner and during focussed group work.'

The recommendation from the EPPE research is that episodes of sustained shared thinking should be encouraged.

These ideas formed the basis for much of the EYFS and can be seen within the Principles into Practice card 4.3: Creativity and Critical Thinking (DCSF, 2008a cited on Foundation Years website 2012). In this card, sustained shared thinking is discussed as:

- **'In the most effective settings practitioners support and challenge children's thinking by getting involved in the thinking process with them.**

- **Sustained shared thinking involves the adult being aware of the children's interests and understandings and the adult and children working together to develop an idea or skill.**

- **Sustained shared thinking can only happen when there are responsive trusting relationships between adults and children.**

- **The adult shows genuine interest, offers encouragement, clarifies ideas and asks open questions. This supports and extends the children's thinking and helps children to make connections in learning.'**

Sustained shared thinking episodes can only take place when the child experiences an adult who is 'tuned in' to them and has a responsive trusting relationship. This forms the foundation of the Key Person relationship. Therefore the Key Person is best placed to support their key children in a sensitive but challenging way, as there is a strong underpinning relationship and an awareness of the child's interests and needs at a deeper level.

The reformed EYFS (DfE 2012) has added the characteristics of effective learning which move through all areas of learning. These are:

- **Playing and exploring**

- **Active learning**

- **Creating and thinking critically**

These expand upon the three Principles into Practice cards:

- **4.1 Play and exploration**

- **4.2 Active learning**

- **4.3 Creativity and critical thinking**

Creating and Thinking Critically is broken down into 3 further components:

- **Having their own ideas – thinking of ideas, finding ways to solve problems, finding new ways to do things**

- **Making links – making links and noticing patterns in their experience, making predictions, testing their ideas, developing ideas of grouping, sequences, cause and effect**

- **Choosing ways to do things – planning, making decisions about how to approach a task, solve a problem and reach a goal, checking how well their activities are going, changing strategies as needed, reviewing how well the approach worked.**

Whilst the Key Person is not identified by the reformed EYFS (DfE 2012) as the best person to think critically with their key children, it is indicated that practitioners should be able to support a range of children in this key skill. However thinking critically is most likely to occur when the child feels settled and secure, and experiences an adult who is attuned to him/her. Attunement, as discussed in chapter 1, occurs when the practitioner is able to respond in a speedy and appropriate manner to the child's communication, both verbal and non-verbal. This in turn requires an adult who is tuned in to the child, and has a responsive, trusting relationship with him/him. Therefore the key person is well placed to support their key child in a sensitive but challenging way, to think critically as there is a strong relationship alongside a deeper knowledge of the child's interests and needs.

How do you 'do' thinking critically?

Creating and thinking critically is stated by the Statutory Framework for the EYFS (DfE 2012) to be when:

> 'Children have and develop their own ideas, make links between ideas, and develop strategies for doing things.'

This goes beyond responding to simple directions such as 'pick up your toys', 'tidy up time' and 'come and get this piece of paper'. Both the child and the practitioner have to take part in the conversation, and extend the ideas and thought within it.

Some of the strategies (Siraj-Blatchford, 2005) to support sustained shared thinking are:

- **Be tuned in to the child you are with, this means listening to the child and responding to their body language and facial cues as well as their words.**

- **Be genuinely interested in what the child says and does, by maintaining eye contact, smiling and nodding and not being distracted by peripheral events.**

- **Respecting the child's ideas, choices and decisions, and inviting them to tell you more about the matter at hand.**

- **Re-capping what the child has said to prompt further thought and discussion.**

- **Offering an experience that relates to the child's discussion and shows continued interest.**

- **Clarifying the ideas that the child has offered.**

- **Suggesting alternative ideas gently and appropriately.**

- **Reminding the child of his/her ideas and thoughts if needed.**

- **Using encouragement to help the child continue his/her thinking and ideas.**

- **Offering an alternative and different viewpoint to challenge the child's thinking.**

- **Speculating and imagining what could happen or what might happen.**

- **Reciprocating the child's ideas and thoughts, by noticing what the child has considered and achieved by thinking ahead.**

- **Asking open questions that have many different answers, rather than asking questions where you may already know the answers.**

- **Modelling the thinking process to the child, by talking about how you have thought a process or idea through.**

Siraj-Blatchford suggests that practitioners consider the type of questioning and commenting they use, and reflect upon whether they use the following:

- **That's an interesting idea**

- **I've never thought of that before**

- **I like what you have done here!**

- **You've made me think**

- **I wonder why…**

Who can think critically with a child?

The EPPE research (Sylva et al 2004) showed that sustained shared thinking is more likely individually with an adult or a peer in focused group work. So while the phrases on the previous page are ones that any practitioner can use with any child, it seems more likely that the child will engage in an episode of thinking critically with a practitioner they know well and trust, and in turn trusts and knows the child well too. As Clarke (2007) states, two key components of sustained shared thinking are:

- **trust and confidence between partners in the situation**

- **time to think, talk and engage with the task.**

Whilst these two important components are more accessible and likely to be in place with a key person and key child relationship, this does not mean thinking critically can only occur within a key person relationship. However it may be more likely to occur particularly for some children who are nervous or unsettled with others.

How do I get opportunities for thinking critically with my key children?

In a similar way with shared care, thinking critically is an opportunity to spend individual, quality time with a key child. There are a number of practical ways in which opportunities for thinking critically can be encouraged:

1. When a child first starts at a setting, it is important that the Key Person gathers information on what parents believe their child is really interested in and loves to think about or talk about. It is important to encourage parents to think broadly about their child's interests and to let you know what they enjoy in play and games, schemas (repeated behaviour patterns that the child may display), songs and dances, media such as television, and even people. These all give the child opportunities to be the expert and lead their Key Person in their ideas and thoughts.

   This information can be gathered in a number of ways, through informal discussions, on induction visits and through home visits.

2. Involve parents in the setting generally so they feel more able to share the details of their child's interests and enthusiasms at home. This involvement of parents has to be carefully considered, to reflect the interests and needs of the parents at your setting.

3. Provide accessible information sheets that show what children are interested in and enjoy so that all practitioners can try to draw upon these opportunities. These can be in the form of fact sheets or passports for each child. These are also very useful for when staff changes occur.

4. Review information on children's interests and passions on a regular basis. This is important to do frequently as children's preferences change at home and at the setting!

5. Share the child's record of learning and development with him or her. This is a good opportunity for thinking critically if the records contain artefacts such as paintings, photographs, mementos from walks and trips out or from home that the child may remember. This presents a real opportunity for the child to be the expert and lead the discussion and thoughts.

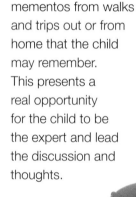

Key messages

- **A child needs a close warm relationship, a Key Person, to enable them to feel secure in each setting they attend.**

- **The Key Person needs to spend time building relationships with the parents of their key children.**

- **The Key Person needs to spend time building relationships with their key children.**

How can I evaluate if there are opportunities for sustained shared thinking at the setting?

Here are a few questions to help you reflect on whether there are opportunities:

* In your setting does each child have a named Key Person?

* How often does each Key Person have opportunities to talk to their key children's parents?

* Does this time include talking about the child's interests and preferences at home?

* How well does each Key Person recognise their key children's high levels of interest and involvement in an activity or experience?

* How well does each Key Person know their key children's interests and preferences?

* How often are the child's learning and development records shared with the child by the Key Person?

* In terms of understanding children's interests and passions, where would each practitioner place the setting on the following scale?

| 1 | 2 | 3 | 4 | 5 | 6 | 7 | 8 | 9 | 10 |

No knowledge of
children's interests

High level of
knowledge of
children's interests

There are no correct answers to these questions, as all settings are different. However hopefully they will allow you to reflect on your practice in relation to shared care, celebrate what is being done well and decide on what needs further development.

Chapter 10

Support and supervision for the Key Person

This chapter considers the issue of support and supervision for the Key Person approach. Supervision is a useful method that can be used in settings to promote an effective Key Person approach by supporting each Key Person emotionally, in their learning and development and reflecting on their ethical approach.

What is supervision?

Supervision is used widely in a range of health, education and social care work, including psychology, mental health, social work, psychotherapy, psychiatry, nursing and therapy. Many of these professions view supervision as an essential part of working effectively with others, and the British Association for Counselling and Psychotherapy (BACP) (2005) adds the idea that supervision should contain support and challenge. Supervision is a mechanism used in what are termed the 'helping professions'.

Scaife (2001) defines supervision as:

'... a formal arrangement to think with one another or others about their work with a view to providing the best possible service ... and enhancing their own personal and professional development.'

So supervision is a tool to give support to the person being supervised. However, experience has shown that the word 'supervision' can be taken to mean the opposite, that the supervisee is not doing their job properly and needs watching! This is an important distinction to understand. Supervision is important for the Key Person approach to work effectively in early years settings, including schools, playgroups, nurseries and childminder networks. Yet in the early years sector and children's centres, experience is that supervision is more likely to be used if the early years practitioners have come from a social work or Family Support background. Supervision may be less likely to be utilised for those from an education or daycare background.

However the Statutory Framework for the EYFS (DfE 2012) emphasises the importance of supervision stating:

'Providers must put appropriate arrangements in place for the supervision of staff who have contact with children and families. Effective supervision provides support, coaching and training for the practitioner and promotes the interest of children. Supervision should foster a culture of mutual support, teamwork and continuous improvement which encourages the confidential discussion of sensitive issues.'

'Supervision should provide opportunities for staff to:

- Discuss any issues – particularly concerning children's development or well-being;

- Identify solutions to address issues as they arise;

- Receive coaching to improve their personal effectiveness.'

This shows an awareness of the importance of supervision for staff to support children and to develop professionally.

Scaife (2001) identifies some common features to show how supervision differs from informal conversations between colleagues. These are:

Consequently, in terms of the Key Person approach, supervision is a planned opportunity for a Key Person to talk on their own or in a small group with their colleague or manager about their key children and families, how they are feeling, and other aspects of their job. This can provide some time to talk about what is going well in addition to what is more challenging. Time for supervision should:

- **be protected**

- **be available on a regular basis (such as monthly)**

- **be requested as needed**

- **have clear rules on what is recorded**

- **have clear rules on who records it and when records are kept**

- **have boundaries of confidentiality**

- **have a clear role of the supervisor and supervisee**

- **Supervision is almost exclusively focused on the needs and experiences of one person, the supervisee, whereas in a conversation there is normally a dialogue and a sharing of the time for both people's needs.**

- **Supervision should not be influenced by other roles the people play in relationship to each other such as manager and staff member, or friends. Obviously supervision often does include other relationships, as described previously, but these should be acknowledged and the implications addressed. In conversations people can slip in and out of different roles.**

- **Supervision should have an agreement or contract (with varying degrees of formality) which specifies the purposes, aims, methods, terms, frequency, and location of the supervision. Conversations are not as formalised in this way.**

- **Supervision serves formative, restorative and normative functions (as discussed below) whereas conversations are open and more general.**

Why is supervision useful?

Supervision is considered useful for a number of reasons, and these tend to be divided into three main areas: Hawkins and Shohet (2006), Kadushin (1976) and Proctor (2001). In terms of the Key Person approach, they are:

1. Educating the Key Person – supervision develops the skills, understanding and abilities of the Key Person, through reflection on and exploration of their work and play with their key children and their key children's parents.

2. Supporting and restoring the Key Person's emotional needs – responding to the Key Person's emotional responses and reactions to their role with their key children and parents, helping reduce stress and feelings of 'burn out'.

3. Giving accountability for the Key Person – the quality control aspect of the supervision, which helps ensure that the role the Key Person plays is appropriate and maintains appropriate ethical standards including safeguarding.

Hawkins and Shohet (2006) emphasise the supportive function of supervision where emotions can be expressed within a safe setting where they can be acknowledged, accepted, reflected upon and learned from. Similarly Steel (2001) suggests that effective supervision allows adults to be psychologically held, listened to and encouraged and also acts as an emotional container for the supervisee.

The Key Person role is an intensive and strongly emotional role, as young children express a lot of strong emotions during their work and play, as do the parents and carers. When a Key Person works and plays with a child with strong feelings, they will absorb some of these strong feelings (as we do when we watch a tear-jerking film and then feel saddened, or talk to a friend on the telephone who is upset). It is important that the Key Person has regular opportunities to talk about these strong feelings and how to manage them.

Supervision can help to reduce stress, as it gives practitioners the opportunity to talk about their feelings of stress and plan how to deal with it. Hawkins and Shohet (2006) use the analogy of 'pit-head time' which the British miners of the 1920s fought for – the right to wash off grime from the pit in work time. Supervision is the equivalent time for the Key Person to wash off their strong feelings from working at the coal-face of their key children and their families' emotions. It is essential for the Key Person to have this time so they are aware of how the children and families they work with affect them and how they are reacting to it. Hawkins and Shohet state that if these emotional needs are not attended to, it can lead to less effective Key People, feelings of stress and in extreme cases burn-out.

Hawkins and Shohet highlight the value of supervision for continued development throughout a person's career and not simply at the beginning:

'We believe that, if the value and experience of good supervision are realised from the beginning of one's professional career, then the 'habit' of receiving good supervision will become an integral part of the work life and the continuing development of the worker.'

In contrast, supervision is not widely used in education and can be greeted with suspicion. Steel (2001) recommends it for teachers working with young people with social, emotional and behavioural difficulties in order to alleviate stress, she states:

'Supervision is a concept that is widely accepted and valued in the social service and nursing sectors, and evidence suggests that the educational field could benefit from adopting it.'

Elfer and Dearnley (2007) state that it can be difficult for nursery staff, particularly from the private, voluntary and independent sector to access any continuing professional development, while Hopkins (1988) emphasises the importance of staff having a regular and consistent place for training discussions. This highlights the difficulties in establishing supervision groups for workers in early years provision but does not mean it is impossible!

Proctor and Inskipp (2001) define the outcome of supervision:

'By good supervision we mean supervision which is satisfying to the participants and to the supervisors and therefore enables the most effective work with clients — the heart of the matter.'

Good supervision should, therefore, be satisfying to the Key Person and the person supervising, which leads to the best and most effective practice for the children and their families – the heart of the matter indeed!

Who can supervise?

Hawkins and Shohet (2006) emphasise that the supervisees and the supervisor need to share enough of a common language and belief system to be able to work and learn together. Scaife (2001) identifies one of the most significant factors for optimum supervision as:

'...the interest that the supervisor has in supervision and in the supervisee. When this is the case, all else is likely to follow.'

For a Key Person, this means the person who supervises them needs to understand what they do in terms of caring for, playing with and working with young children and working in partnership with parents. It could be a colleague or a manager or someone who understands the work context.

Open-door policies

In many settings managers have an 'open-door' policy for staff. However, this alone is not as effective as having a structured system of supervision. The Key Person approach is about developing strong positive relationships with a small group of children and their families. Therefore a Key Person too, needs to have someone they can have a strong positive relationship with, so that they can turn to them on a planned regular basis to share how they are feeling, raise concerns, celebrate good work and generally talk things through. This doesn't always happen through having an 'open door'. Supervision gives a space and time to talk that is protected for each Key Person. Often supervision sessions begin by practitioners saying they have nothing to share, but by the end of the time allocated there has been lots to talk about and the practitioner feels much better about their role.

Are there different types of supervision?

Often supervision is individual, in which a Key Person sits and talks with a colleague, a senior colleague or a manager. Within this there is vertical and horizontal supervision. Hawkins and Shohet (2006) explain that:

- **Vertical supervision occurs where a more experienced supervisor works with a less experienced supervisee, so occurs where a new practitioner is supervised by a more established Senior colleague.**

- **Horizontal supervision occurs where the supervisor and supervisee are on the same level and are colleagues on an equal footing and status.**

Supervision can also be undertaken in a group, but the group needs to be small, with no more than six to eight people involved. If groups are too big, then the practitioners are less willing to talk, or listen to each other, or are worried to talk and show vulnerabilities. However one approach to group supervision could be for a small group of practitioners to agree to discuss one or two focus children or parents who staff are finding challenging. There need to be clear rules on how the group is going to operate which the group work together to create. This would include how often the group is going to meet, when, where, for how long and importantly confidentiality. It may also be useful to encourage openness and honesty as this may be a new approach to a staff group. It is important to link the rules of group supervision to safeguarding policies so everyone understands the limits to confidentiality.

Key messages

- **Supervision can play an important part in supporting practitioners to be effective as Key People to their key children.**

- **Supervision plays a role in supporting the learning and development and emotions involved in being a Key Person.**

- **Supervision can support practitioners in maintaining an ethical approach to their work and play as Key People.**

- **Supervision can be established in different ways in the early years setting to support an effective Key Person approach.**

How can I evaluate if there are opportunities to support practitioners at the setting in the Key Person approach?

Here are a few questions to help you reflect on whether there are opportunities:

✳ In your setting does each child have a named Key Person?

✳ How often does each Key Person have opportunities to talk with another practitioner or manager in the setting about how things are going with their key children?

✳ How often does each Key Person have opportunities to talk with another practitioner or manager in the setting about how things are going with their key children's parents?

✳ Does this time include talking about how the Key Person feels about each key child and/or parent?

✳ Does this time include talking about how the Key Person has learned and developed from their work with each key child and/or parent?

✳ How well supported does each Key Person feel in delivering an effective Key Person approach to their key children and/or parents?

✳ In terms of feeling supported in working within the Key Person approach, where would each practitioner place themselves on the following scale?

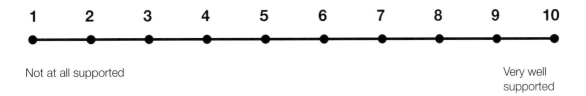

| 1 | 2 | 3 | 4 | 5 | 6 | 7 | 8 | 9 | 10 |

Not at all supported

Very well supported

There are no correct answers to these questions, as all settings are different. However hopefully they will allow you to reflect on your practice in relation to shared care, celebrate what is being done well and decide on what needs further development.

Chapter 11

Challenges and solutions

It is important to acknowledge that while the Key Person approach has numerous benefits, there are also some challenges to face. In this chapter we outline each challenge in a brief scenario. It is followed by a discussion of why this may come about and possible solutions. There are photocopies of these scenarios available in the photocopiable resources section on pages 92-96. You can use these with staff to brainstorm solutions in staff meetings or during other staff development opportunities.

Challenge

You can't have a Key Person approach in an out-of-school care setting because the child already has a Key Person in their Reception or nursery class.

Zoe has a Key Person, Miss Smith, in her nursery class. Zoe has built a warm relationship with Miss Smith in nursery, but now needs to go to the out-of-school club because her Mum is working longer hours. Does Zoe need a new Key Person in the out-of-school club?

Questions to consider:

- **Can a child have more than one Key person in their life?**

- **Does a child need a Key Person in every part of their life?**

Remember that babies and young children can have a few close relationships and that the relationship with the Key Person does not affect other close relationships with the family.

Remember that a child needs a close warm relationship to enable them to feel secure in each setting they attend.

Possible solutions

Zoe is unlikely to feel secure in the out-of-school club with staff that she has not met before, even if she has a close relationship with Miss Smith in the nursery class. This is because she is not able to go to Miss Smith in the out-of-school club because Miss Smith doesn't work there. Zoe will need a Key Person in the out-of-school club, and as Miss Smith has a wealth of knowledge about Zoe, with Zoe's parents' consent she could share some key information alongside Zoe's parents with the out-of-school club.

It will also be important for Miss Smith to pass any relevant information about Zoe's day to the out-of-school club so that Zoe has a smooth transition.

Challenge

You can't have a Key Person approach in an out-of-school setting because it would involve staff writing observations and individual learning journey books for each child in the Foundation Stage.

Nathaniel is attending an out-of-school club after attending his Reception class. His teacher, Mr Patel, is keeping a learning journey for Nathaniel. Does Nathaniel need another Key Person as well as Mr. Patel? Does he need another learning journey?

Questions to consider:

- **Can a child have more than one Key Person in their life?**

- **Does a child need a Key person in every part of his life?**

- **Does a child need a learning journey and observations collated by his Key person from his out-of-school club?**

Remember that babies and young children can have a few close relationships and that the relationship with the Key Person does not affect other close relationships with the family.

Remember that a child needs a close warm relationship to enable them to feel secure in each setting they attend.

Possible solutions

Nathaniel, like Zoe, is unlikely to feel secure in the out-of-school club unless there are familiar staff there with whom he has developed a relationship. It will be important for Nathaniel to have a named Key Person so he has someone he can turn to and depend on. The out-of-school club decide Sharon is the best key person for Nathaniel as she is there on the same sessions as him and generally works and plays with the younger children.

Since Mr. Patel, Nathaniel's teacher is keeping a learning journey, it would be ideal if Sharon could share her observations from the out-of-school club on a regular basis with Mr. Patel. To do this she would need consent from Nathaniel's parents. This would lead to Nathaniel's learning journey in school having a more rounded picture of Nathaniel as it contains observations, photographs and pictures from Nathaniel in a range of settings, including school and the out-of-school club. The Statutory Framework for the EYFS (DfE 2012) states that wrap around care should be guided by the learning and development requirements. Practitioners should seek to complement learning in settings in which children spend more time.

Challenge

You can't have a Key Person approach as it worries the parents that their child may become more attached to their Key Person than to them as parents.

Maisie has recently started going to Selina, a childminder, and has settled in well. However Maisie has now started to cry when her parents come to collect her at the end of the day to take her home. This is worrying Maisie's mum who doesn't like to see her daughter getting upset.

Questions to consider:

- **Can a child have a close relationship with her Key Person and her parents?**

- **Can a Key Person build a relationship with a child without building a relationship with the child's parents?**

Remember that the Key Person needs to spend time building relationships with the parents of their key children.

Remember that babies and young children can have a few close relationships and that the relationship with the Key Person does not affect other close relationships with the family.

Possible solutions

Selina has developed a close relationship with Maisie through playing and spending time with her. The relationship has developed well and Selina needs to ensure she has an equally strong relationship with Maisie's mum. This means Selina needs to spend time with Maisie's mum explaining how her role as a childminder does not affect Maisie's relationship with her parents. It may be useful for Selina to explain that Maisie has the capacity to have more than one positive relationship/attachment at a time. A useful analogy can be to explain how a young child can build up strong relationships with a number of family members including parents, grandparents and siblings.

It will also be important for Selina to be sensitive to Maisie's mum's feelings and recognise how Maisie's crying may make her feel. She also could share photographs of Maisie from her learning journey to show how Maisie enjoys her time with Selina and to help Maisie's mum feel part of her day.

Challenge

You can't have a Key Person approach because practitioners may become over attached to their key children.

Jamie has been in Toddlers for six months. He has a warm positive relationship with his Key Person, Danielle. Jamie is very keen to be with Danielle and gets upset when Danielle takes her lunch break. Danielle tends to cut her lunch short so that she can calm Jamie down. In addition Danielle is not keen to attend courses. While she realises that the courses may be helpful and give her further ideas on working with the toddlers, she worries that Jamie will get upset without her and other staff won't know how to comfort him.

Questions to consider:

- **Can a Key Person be effective without a supportive manager and support systems such as regular supervision?**

- **Is it fair on practitioners and children to have a Key Person approach without a 'buddy' Key Person?**

Remember that a Key Person needs to have a 'buddy' Key Person in settings other than childminders. This is what is encouraged in Development Matters in the EYFS (Early Education 2012).

Remember that an effective Key Person is part of a wider team and needs to access regular supervision and support from the senior staff or manager.

Possible solutions

Danielle needs support in two forms from the nursery in which she works. She needs to have a 'buddy' Key Person who can support Jamie at times such as during her lunch break and training days. This should be another member of staff such as Lisa from the Toddler room. It will be important that Danielle helps Jamie to build up the relationship with Lisa. She can do this by sharing information about Jamie, his care routines and his likes and dislikes and also encouraging Jamie to spend time with Lisa, preferably during activities where he feels safe and secure (rather than care routines initially).

Danielle will also benefit from regular opportunities to talk with her room leader or manager during supervision sessions about how she is getting along with all her key children. This will allow time to talk about professional boundaries as well as the strong feelings evoked through working with babies and young children.

Challenge

You can't have a Key Person approach because the child may become too dependent on their Key Person.

Lila has been in the Baby room for four weeks. She bonded well with Richard her Key Person. Lila is very keen to be with Richard and gets upset when Richard is with other children or goes out of the room. Richard is a new practitioner in the Baby room and finds Lila quite demanding at times.

Possible solutions

Richard is empathetic, sensitive and responsive to Lila's needs and feelings and has therefore developed a strong relationship with her. However it is important that Richard has time and opportunity to share his feelings about his key children on a regular basis through supervision from his manager or room leader. This would allow Richard time to 'unload' about how he is feeling about Lila. Now that Lila is settled it would be useful to introduce the 'buddy' Key Person to Lila on a more regular basis at times where Lila feels safe and secure. This may be during times for play and exploration rather than care routines until Lila is ready for this.

It is important that Richard has trust in the 'buddy' Key person as Lila will pick up on his feelings about this staff member. Sian is selected as a 'buddy' Key Person as she also works in the baby room, Richard knows her well and Lila has shown a liking for her. This will allow Richard to feel more confident to get Sian to step in when he needs to go for his break or leave the room.

Questions to consider:

- **Can a Key Person be effective without a supportive manager and support systems such as regular supervision?**

- **Is it fair on practitioners and children to have a Key Person approach without a 'buddy' Key Person?**

- **Can a Key Person build a relationship with a child without building a relationship with the child's parents?**

Remember that a Key Person needs to have a 'buddy' Key Person in settings other than childminders.

Remember that an effective Key Person is part of a wider team and needs to access regular supervision and support from the senior staff or manager.

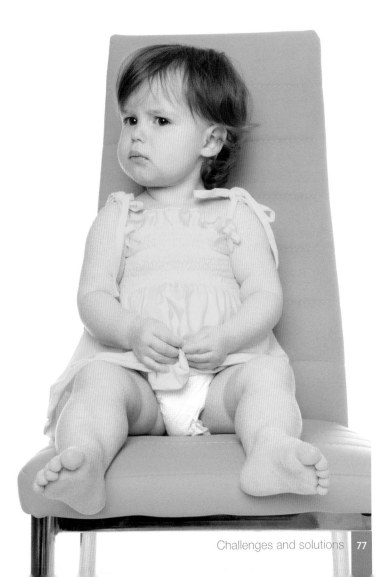

Challenge

You can't have a Key Person approach as children become attached to their Key Person but still have to move to new rooms or new settings.

Jasmine attends the mixed-age playgroup, Busy Fingers, and is only going to be there for a year. This is unlike other children who attend for two or more years. The manager and staff are discussing whether Jasmine needs a Key Person as she seems very confident and is one of the oldest children at nearly four. She is due to go to Reception after spending her year in Busy Fingers.

Questions to consider:

- **Can a child have more than one Key Person in their life?**

- **Does a child need a Key Person in every part of their life?**

Remember that the Statutory Framework for the Early Years Foundation Stage (DfE 2012) sets a statutory requirement that every child has a key person.

Remember that a child's need for the Key Person approach does not end at a certain age within the EYFS but is needed throughout from birth to the end of Reception.

Remember the Statutory Framework for the EYFS (DfE 2012) states:

'Each child must be assigned a key person. Their role is to help ensure that every child's care is tailored to meet their individual needs, to help the child become familiar with the setting, offer a settled relationship for the child and build a relationship with the parents.'
(page 18, DfE, 2012)

Possible solutions

This all shows that Jasmine is entitled to a Key Person even though she is attending the setting for a shorter time than other children.

In addition the Key Person Principles into Practice card (DCSF 2008a cited on Foundation Years website 2012) states:

'Even when children are older and can hold special people in mind for longer there is still a need for them to have a key person to depend on in the setting, such as their teacher or a teaching assistant' (Foundation Years website, 2012)

Children are entitled to a Key Person throughout their time in the EYFS, even as they approach four or five years of age.

Challenge

You can't have a Key Person approach because there is no way you can be there all the time for your key children – you may not be working when they arrive in the morning or you may have gone home from your shift when they go home at night.

Alisha attends a day nursery, Happy People, and does long hours on the three days she attends due to her parents' work shifts as nurses and the distance they travel to work. Alisha arrives at nursery at 7.30am and leaves at 6pm. Her Key Person Sally does the morning shift and is there to open the nursery at 7.15am and finishes work at 3pm each day. Alisha has been at the nursery for a couple of weeks and is still a little unsettled.

Questions to consider:

- **Can a child have more than one Key Person in their life?**

- **Is it fair on practitioners and children to have a Key Person approach without a 'buddy' Key Person?**

- **Can a Key Person build a relationship with a child without building a relationship with the child's parents?**

Remember that the Key Person needs to spend time building relationships with the parents of their key children.

Remember that a Key Person needs to have a 'buddy' Key Person in settings other than childminders.

Possible solutions

Sally has begun to develop a relationship with Alisha but she is struggling as she is not available at work for the same hours as Alisha attends. This makes it harder for Alisha to settle and trust Sally and also for Sally to build up a positive relationship with Alisha. Sally needs to have a 'buddy' Key Person for Alisha who works the other part of Alisha's day at Happy People. Danni works in the same room as Sally and is there at the end of the working day until 6pm. Although Alisha has not yet bonded with Sally fully and has not spent much time with Danni, it seems a good idea to have Danni as the 'buddy' Key Person. This means that in the afternoon when Sally is about to go home, she says goodbye to Alisha and lets her know that Danni is there to look after her.

Sally meets with Alisha's parents, introduces Danni to them and explains that Danni is to be Alisha's 'buddy' Key Person. She explains how their roles work together and that Danni will be able to greet them and tell them how Alisha has been during the day at nursery. Danni takes over Alisha's care routines after 3pm and also tries to spend time with Alisha playing while Sally is still there before 3pm.

Challenge

You can't have a Key Person approach as you have to work as part of a team and otherwise practitioners may say 'That's not my key child so I am not changing their nappy'.

Zane attends a set-up and pack-away playgroup, Jellytots, in the local church hall. He has developed a good relationship with Leah and is happy to attend playgroup. There have been a few staffing changes as a couple of staff have left and one long-standing member of staff has gone on maternity leave. The new members of staff are not familiar with the Key Person approach and have used a rotation approach for care routines. They believe that the children should learn to get along with everyone.

Questions to consider

- **Can a child have more than one Key Person in their life?**

- **Does a child need a Key Person in every part of their life?**

Remember that an effective Key Person is part of a wider team and needs access to regular supervision and support from the senior staff or manager.

Remember that the Key Person approach has to be part of the whole setting's approaches and policies and can't be done by one member of staff on their own.

Remember that the Statutory Framework for the Early Years Foundation Stage (DfE, 2012) sets a statutory requirement that every child has a key person.

Possible solutions

Zane has settled well at the playgroup Jellytots. However it is important to remember that the Statutory Framework for the EYFS sets a statutory requirement that every child has a Key Person as a minimum requirement. This therefore cannot be ignored. However it is important that the new staff develop an understanding of the Key Person approach and why it is important to young children to have a warm, trusting relationship that they can depend on. It may be useful to spend some staff-meeting time talking about what the staff think a Key Person should do and how it can work at Jellytots. This could be used as the basis for a Key Person policy which can be shared with parents and children.

Challenge

You can't have a Key Person approach in Reception because there are too many children and the children have to get ready for Year 1.

Jameel is about to start his second term in Reception class and turned five years old in October. He is in a class of 30. His previous teacher, Mrs Wills, is leaving for a new job. The teaching assistant, Miss Smith, has stayed with the class. A new teacher, Mrs Carr is taking over the class in January and is discussing with the Foundation Stage Coordinator and the teaching assistant whether it is worth allocating the children to a new Key Person as they have only got seven months in Reception before they move into Year 1.

Questions to consider

- **Does a child need a Key Person in every part of his life?**

- **Does a child in Reception need a Key Person?**

Remember that the Statutory Framework for the EYFS (DfE 2012) sets a statutory requirement that every child has a Key Person. Remember that a child's need for the Key Person approach does not end at a certain age within the EYFS but is needed, throughout from birth to the end of Reception.

Possible solutions

Although Jameel is over five years old, he is still entitled to a Key Person as a legal requirement of the EYFS Statutory Framework (DfE 2012). Either Mrs Carr or Miss Smith will be Jameel's Key Person. If Jameel had developed a positive relationship with Miss Smith, the teaching assistant, it would be preferable to allocate Jameel to Miss Smith. However there needs to be a discussion as to who the children have developed a stronger relationship with, preferably with Mrs Wills so that she can share her views and opinions. All the children in Reception benefit from knowing they have a Key Person to turn to in times of need for the remainder of their time in Reception and ideally beyond.

Challenge

You can't have a Key Person approach because practitioners shouldn't have special children and should treat children all the same.

Natysha is in Marianne's key group and has been for some time. Marianne has a close relationship with Natysha and knows Natysha's mum very well. Another practitioner, Tanya, in the same room feels that Marianne favours Natysha over other children, fussing over her and keeping her on her knee for too long and not allowing her to explore. Tanya takes the issue up with her manager and says she feels the Key Person system is promoting staff favouring certain children.

Questions to consider:

- **Can a Key Person be effective without a supportive manager and support systems such as regular supervision?**

- **Is it fair on practitioners and children to have a Key Person approach without a 'buddy' Key Person?**

Can a Key Person build a relationship with a child without building a relationship with the child's parents?

Remember that a Key Person needs to have a 'buddy' Key Person in settings other than childminders.

Remember that an effective Key Person is part of a wider team and needs to access regular supervision and support from the senior staff or manager.

Possible solutions

While this initially may seem to be an issue concerning Tanya and Marianne, it relates to the smooth running of the Key Person approach. It is important that Marianne accesses regular supervision with her manager to discuss how she is feeling about the children in her group and whether she is allowing them to feel secure, know where to seek comfort but also be able to explore and investigate independently. It will be important that this issue is discussed in supervision, but it may also require a wider discussion on the Key Person approach within a whole staff meeting. Within the policy it will also be useful to have guidance on professional and personal boundaries to ensure that staff are clear.

Reflecting on practice

This chapter provides a number of activities which can be undertaken by early years settings in order to evaluate the effectiveness of their Key Person approach. It uses an action research approach with all relevant stakeholders:

* managers/leaders
* staff to reflect on their practice
* parents
* children.

The Foundation Years website (2012) encourages the use of reflection using the Principles into Practice Key Person card (DCSF 2008a).

Evaluate your current practice within the Key Person approach through examination of rotas, policy and discussion with staff.

Do you have a Key Person for each child?

Once it is established whether each child has a Key Person, it is important to check whether the named staff member is present and working when their key children are present. This is more relevant in settings where the staff work shifts and may not be at the setting when the child is there. It is impossible for a Key Person to do exactly the same hours as all their key children but they do need time to build a relationship and play together. If a child is only there for a short period per week, this proportion of time needs to become higher. So for a child who only attends for one or two sessions or a few hours a week, it is important to check that their Key Person is there for most of their sessions or hours.

Activity

Note all the children's names and see if their Key Person is there for the majority (above 50 per cent) of their hours.

Do the staff at the setting have a shared understanding of the Key Person approach?

The Key Person approach has to be a whole-setting approach where staff have a shared understanding of what this means. It is useful to ask staff questions to check their understanding and revisit this at regular opportunities or when new staff join the setting.

Activity

Ask the staff to write down:

* the main roles of the Key Person
* the main activities that the Key Person should do with their key children (for example, observation, making learning journals, spending time playing, care routines, paperwork, planning, sharing information with parents).

The staff responses can lead to a discussion and then an agreed policy on the roles and responsibilities of the Key Person in the setting.

How well does each Key Person know their key children?

In order for the Key Person approach to work, staff have to know all of their Key Children.

> ### Activity
>
> Ask each Key Person to write down the names of all their Key Children.

This is a useful activity to do, as sometimes staff can't remember all their Key Children when asked. If any child is forgotten it is important for the Key Person to ensure they spend more time with them regularly. It can often be children who attend the setting on a part-time basis or children who are neither very quiet or very demanding, but fall in between, who get less attention.

If staff can name all their Key Children, then the next activity is helpful:

> ### Activities
>
> - Ask each Key Person to write three special things about each key child. This can include the child's favourite toys, details of family or current interests.
>
> - Use the scenarios within the photocopiable resources section on pages 92-96 to promote discussion amongst staff during a staff meeting. It is important to choose scenarios that are relevant to your early years setting, and allow time for staff to talk. Our suggested answers are shown in Chapter 11, but it is important for staff to consider and reflect upon their own answers.

> ### Activity
>
> Give each staff member a photocopy of the Key Person question sheet on page 90 and the blank evidence sheet on page 91 to complete. This will provide a way of helping staff to reflect upon the Key Person approach and evaluate their practice. It is important to allow time for staff to share their answers and thoughts. The collated evidence from the staff will show the effective practice in place already and where evidence is lacking this will show where further development and support is needed.
>
> Take, for example, the question: How do you support children's transitions between Key Person relationships in the setting when there are staff changes? Evidence for this could include:
>
> - **The new Key Person visits the child in their new room.**
>
> - **Parents are invited in to be introduced to the new Key Person and to see the new room.**
>
> - **A transition form on each child is completed by the current Key Person.**
>
> - **The child visits the new room and meets their Key Person on regular occasions before moving.**

How well does each Key Person know their Key Children's families and carers?

As discussed previously in the book it is important for the Key Person to build a relationship with the parents/carers and family. This can be more difficult for some practitioners who find parent partnership a challenging part of their Key Person role. The following activity is useful:

> ### Activity
>
> Ask each Key Person to name all their Key Children's parents or carers.

This can lead to much discussion as it can be difficult for practitioners to suddenly start using parents' and carers' names, so it provides encouragement for practitioners to ask parents and carers what they would prefer to be called. If staff are able to name their key children's parents and carers then the following activity is useful:

> ### Activity
>
> Ask each Key Person to name one special thing about their key child's parents, carers or family (this includes family members' jobs, professions, interests or hobbies).

Evaluate your current practice within the Key Person approach working directly with parents

In order to find out if the Key Person approach is working in your setting, it is important to find out if parents have an understanding of the Key Person approach.

Activities

- Ask the parents to name their child's Key Person.

- Ask the parents if they understand what their Key Person does with their child.

- Ask the parents if they can know one special thing about their Key Person.

This can be done through questionnaires (although these need to be short and manageable). It may be easier to simply ask parents, or you can use more creative ways of gaining the information such as asking parents to put their child's name on the correct photograph.

Evaluate your current practice within the Key Person approach working directly with children

Activities

- Ask the children to name their Key Person.

- Ask the children if they can explain what their Key Person does with them.

- Ask the children if they know one special thing about their Key Person.

This can be done verbally with older children. However with younger children or children who have difficulties with language, it can be useful to have staff photographs for children to point to for the first question. For the youngest children and babies it is useful to use observation of children's eye gaze and behaviour to answer the first question. It can be through observing who the child likes to go to, looks at or puts their arms up to that will show if they have developed a bond with their Key Person. For the third question, objects of reference, such as nappies, dinner plates or photographs can be used to help ask children what their Key Person does with them but this will have challenges as younger children may prefer to play with the items!

ACCAC (Qualifications, Curriculum and Assessment Authority for Wales) (2000) *Desirable Outcomes for Children's Learning before Compulsory School Age* (www.wales.gov.uk).

Ainsworth, M., Blehar, M., Waters, E., and Wall, S., (1978) *Patterns of attachment*, Hillsdale, NJ: Lawrence Erlbaum and Associates.

Belsky, J., (2006) 'Early child care and early child development: major findings of the NICHD study of early child care', *European Journal of Developmental Psychology*, 3(1), pp.95-110.

Belsky, J., and Fearon, R. M. P., (2002) 'Early attachment security, subsequent maternal sensitivity, and later child development: does continuity in development depend upon continuity of caregiving?' *Attachment and Human Development*, 4(3), pp.361-387.

Belsky, J., Burchinal, M., Mc Cartney, K., Vandell, D. L., Clarke-Stewart, K. A., and Owen, M. T., (2007) 'Are there long-term effects of early child care?' *Child Development*, 78(2), pp.681- 701.

Bowlby, J., (1953) *Child Care and the Growth of Love*. Harmondsworth: Penguin.

Bowlby, J., (1969) *Attachment and Loss Volume 1: Attachment*, New York: Basic Books.

Bowlby, J., (1973) *Attachment and Loss Volume 2: Separation*, New York: Basic Books.

Bowlby, J., (1980) *Attachment and Loss Volume 3: Loss*, New York: Basic Books.

Clarke, J (2007) *Sustained Shared Thinking*, London: Featherstone Education, Bloomsbury Publishing.

David, T., Goouch, K., Powell, S. and Abbott, L. (2003) *Birth to Three Matters: A Review of the Literature* (Research Report Number 444), Nottingham, Queen's Printer/DfES.

De Rosnay, M., and Harris, P. (2002) 'Individual differences in children's understanding of emotion: the roles of attachment and language', *Attachment and Human Development* 41, pp.39-54.

DCSF (2008a) *The Early Years Foundation Stage*, Nottingham: DCSF Publications.

DCSF (2008b) *Social and Emotional Aspects of Development*, Nottingham: DCSF Publications.

DCSF (2010) *Working Together to Safeguard Children - a guide to inter-agency working to safeguard and promote the welfare of children*, Nottingham: DCSF Publications.

DfE (2012) *Statutory Framework for the EYFS*, www.dfe.gov.uk accessed 31.3.12

DfES (2007) *Creating the Picture*, DfES Publications.

Dunn, J. (1993) *Young Children's Close Relationships: Beyond Attachment*, Newbury Park California: Sage

Early Education (2012) *Development Matters in the EYFS*, www.early-education.org.uk accessed 31.3.12

Education and Training Inspectorate (ETI) (2004) Together Towards Improvement: *A Process for Self-Evaluation – Pre-school Education* (www.etini.gov.uk).

Elfer, P. and Dearnley, K. (2007) 'Nurseries and emotional well-being: evaluating an emotionally containing model of continuing professional development', *Early Years*, 27 (3), pp.267-80

Elfer, P., Goldschmied, E. and Selleck, D. (2003) *Key Persons in the Nursery: Building relationships for quality provision*, Oxon: David Fulton Publishers.

Evangelou, M., Sylva, K., Kyriacou, M., Wild, M. and Glenny, G. (2009) *Early Years Learning and Development Review*, Research Report DCSF-RR176, DCSF/University of Oxford.

Featherstone, S. and Bayley, R. (2001) *Foundations for Independence, Developing Independent Learning in the Foundation Stage*, London: Featherstone Education, Bloomsbury Publishing.

Foundation Years (2012) *Overall reforms to the 2012 EYFS framework*, www.foundationyears.org.uk accessed 31.3.12

Foundation Years (2012) *Getting ready for the revised EYFS Learning Environment*, www.foundationyears.org.uk accessed 31.3.12

Foundation Years (2012) *Getting Ready for the revised EYFS Time to reflect*, www.foundationyears.org.uk accessed 31.3.12

Foundation Years (2012) *Top tips on getting ready for EYFS*, www.foundationyears.org.uk accessed 31.3.12

Foundation Years (2012) *Frequently asked questions on the new EYFS*, www.foundationyears.org.uk accessed 31.3.12

Gerhardt, S. (2004) *Why Love Matters: How affection shapes the baby's brain*, Hove: Routledge.

Goldschmeid, E. and Jackson, S. (1994) *People Under Three: Young Children in Day Care*, London: Routledge.

Goldschmied, E. and Selleck, D. (1996) *Communication Between Babies in Their First Year*. London: National Children's Bureau Early Childhood Unit.

Grenier, J. (1999) '*All about...Developing positive relationships with children*', Nursery World, 16th September, pp.12-13 cited in the EYFS (2007) CD-ROM information.

Hawkins and Shohet (2006) *Supervision in the Helping Professions* (3rd ed), Maidenhead: Open University Press/McGraw-Hill Publications.

Hopkins, (1988) 'Facilitating the development of intimacy between nurses and infants in day nurseries', *Early Child Development and Care*, 33, pp. 99-111.

Howes, C. (1999) *Attachment relationships in the context of multiple carers*. In Cassidy, J. and Shaver, P.R. (eds) Handbook of Attachment, New York: The Guildford Press, pp.671-687.

Johnson, B. and Howard, S. (1999) 'Resilience – a Slippery Concept', *AEU (SA Branch) Journal* May: 26 (8)

Kadushin, A. (1976) *Supervision in Social Work*, New York: Columbia University Press.

Laevers, F. (1994) 'A Process-Oriented Child Monitoring System' (www.cego.be).

Laible, D.J., and Thompson, R. A. (2000) 'Mother-child discourse, attachment security, shared positive affect and early conscience development', *Child development*, 71(5) pp.1424-1440.

Learning and Teaching Scotland (2010) *Pre-Birth to Three Positive Outcomes for Scotland's Children and Families* (www.ltscotland.org.uk).

Karmiloff-Smith, A. (1994) *Baby It's You*, London: Ebury Press.

Kochanska, G. (2001) 'Emotional development in children with different attachment histories: The first three years', *Child Development*, 72(2) pp.474-491.

Kochanska, G. (2002) 'Mutually responsive orientation between mothers and their young children: a context for the early development of conscience', *Current Directions in Psychological Science*. 11(6) pp.191-195.

Kochanska, G., Aksan, N., Knaack A., and Rhines, H.M. (2004) 'Maternal parenting and children's conscience: early security as moderator', *Child development* 75(4) pp.1229-1242.

National Institute of Child Health and Human Development (NICHD) Early Childcare Research Network (1996) 'Characteristics of infant childcare: factors contributing to positive caregiving', *Early Childhood Research Quarterly* 11: pp.269-306.

National Scientific Council on the Developing Child (2007) 'The Timing and Quality of Early Experiences Combine to Shape Brain Architecture': Working Paper No. 5 (www.developingchild.net).

NCB (2012) *A Know how guide: The EYFS progress check at age two*, www.foundationyears.org.uk accessed 31.3.12

Northern Ireland Council for the Curriculum, Examinations and Assessment (2006) *Curricular Guidance for Pre-school Education* (www.nicurriculum.org.uk).

Plymouth Safeguarding Board (2010) Serious Case Review Overview Report Executive Summary in respect of Nursery Z (www.plymouth.gov.uk/.../childrensocialcare/localsafeguardingchildrenboard).

Proctor, B. and Inskipp, F. (2001) 'Group supervision' in Scaife, J. *Supervision in the Mental Health Professions: A Practitioner's Guide*, Hove: Routledge.

Roberts, R. (2002) *Developing Self-esteem and Early Learning in Young Children*, London: Paul Chapman/Sage.
Roberts, R (2010) *Wellbeing from Birth*, London: Sage Publications.

Robinson, M. (2003) *From Birth to One – The Year of Opportunity*, Buckingham: Open University Press.

Rutter, M., Beckett, C., Castle, J., Colvert, E., Kreppner, J., Mehta, M., Stevens, S., and Sonuga-Barke, E. (2007) 'Effects of a profound early institutional deprivation: An overview of findings from a UK longitudinal study of Romanian adoptees', *European Journal of Developmental Psychology*. 4(3) pp.332-350.

Scaife, J. (2001) *Supervision in the Mental Health Professions: A Practitioner's Guide*, Hove: Routledge.

Scottish Executive (2004) *A Curriculum for Excellence* (www.ltscotland.org.uk).

Scottish Executive (2006) *Building the curriculum 1 – the contribution of curriculum areas* (www.ltscotland.org.uk).

Scottish Executive (2007) *Building the curriculum 2 – active learning in the early years* (www.ltscotland.org.uk).

Scottish Government (2008a) *The Early Years Framework* (www.scotland.gov.uk).

Scottish Government (2008b) *Achieving Our Potential* (www.scotland.gov.uk).

Scottish Government (2008c) *Equally Well* (www.scotland.gov.uk).

Scottish Government (2008d) *Getting It Right for Every Child* (www.scotland.gov.uk).

Selleck (2001) 'Being Under 3 Years of Age: Enhancing Quality Experiences' in Pugh, G. (ed) (2001) *Contemporary Issues in the Early Years*, Third Edition, London: Paul Chapman Publishing.

Selleck, D. and Griffin, S. (1996) 'Quality for the Under Threes' in Pugh, G. (ed) *Contemporary Issues in the Early Years* (2nd edition), London: Paul Chapman/Sage pp.152-169.

Siraj-Blatchford, I. (2005) 'Birth to Eight Matters! Seeking Seamlessness – Continuity? Integration? Creativity? Quality Interactions Matter' Presentation to TACTYC Annual Conference (www.tactyc.org.uk/pdfs/2005conf_siraj.pdf).

Siraj-Blatchford, I., Sylva, K., Muttock, S., Gilden, R. and Bell, D. (2002). *Researching Effective Pedagogy in the Early Years*. London: Department for Education and Skills, Research Report 356.

Sroufe, L. A., Egeland, B., Carson, A. and Collins, W. A. (2005). *The Development of the Person. The Minnesota Study of Risk and Adaptation from Birth to Adulthood*, NY and London: The Guildford Press.

Steel, L. (2001) 'Staff Support through Supervision', *Emotional and Behavioural Difficulties*, 6 (2), pp.91-101.

Sure Start (2003) *Birth to Three Matters* framework (www.education.gov.uk).

Sure Start (2006) *Personal, Social and Emotional Development (PSED) Training materials birth to five* (www.surestart.gov.uk).

Sylva, K. Melhuish, E., Sammons, P., Siraj-Blatchford, I. & Taggart, B. (2004) *The Effective Provision of Pre-school Education (EPPE) Project: Findings from Pre-school to end of Key Stage 1*, DfES Publications, (www.education.gov.uk/publications/eOrderingDownload/SSU-SF-2004-01.pdf).

Sylva, K., Melhuish, E., Sammons, P., Siraj-Blatchford, I., and Taggart, B. (2008) *Effective Pre-school and Primary Education 3-11 Project (EPPE 3-11) Final report from the primary phase: Pre-school, school and family influences on children's development during Key Stage 2 (Age 7-11)*, (Research Report), Nottingham: DCSF Publications.

Thompson, R. A. (2000) 'The legacy of early attachments', *Child Development* 71(1) pp.145-152.

Trevarthen, C. (1988) 'Universal cooperative motives: How infants begin to know language and skills in culture' in Jahoda, G. and Lewis, I.M. (eds) *Acquiring Culture: Cross-Cultural Studies in Child Development*, pp.37-90, Croom Helm.

Vygotsky, L. (1962) *Thought and Language*, Cambridge, Mass.

Welsh Assembly Government (WAG) (2008a) *A Framework for Children's Learning for 3-7 year olds in Wales* (www.wales.gov.uk).

Welsh Assembly Government (WAG) (2008b) Skills Framework for 3 to 19 year olds in Wales (www.wales.gov.uk).

Welsh Assembly Government (WAG) (2008c) *Observing Children* (www.wales.gov.uk).

Welsh Assembly Government (WAG) (2008d) *Learning and Teaching Pedagogy* (www.wales.gov.uk).

1 In what ways do you build a genuine bond with each child and their family? Think of each of your key children in turn.	**2** How do you help your key children become familiar with the environment and feel safe in it?	**3** How do you ensure that each key child's records of progress and development are created and shared by parents, the child, the key person and other professionals? When does this happen? How often?	**4** How do you support your key children in exploring new experiences and activities? Who needs more support in new experiences? How do you know?
5 How do you ensure you respond sensitively to each of your key children's feelings, ideas and behaviour? Consider each of your key children in turn.	**6** What support is available for practitioners in your setting who start to feel too attached to a key child?	**7** How do you reassure other staff and parents that children will not become too dependent on their Key Person?	**8** When do you talk to the parents of your key children so you know how to care for them? How often does this happen? Is it on a regular basis?
9 How do you support children and parents in transitions? Are they given time with and information about their new Key Person when they move rooms or settings?	**A Key Person has special responsibilities for working with a small number of children, giving them the reassurance to feel safe and cared for and building relationships with their parents.**		**10** How do you show that you recognise that children and babies are likely to be less independent in new situations or when unwell or anxious? How do you support this?
11 How do you try to ensure each child can be reassured and comforted by key adults at times when they may need it?	**12** Who is the Key Person for each child? When does the Key Person spend time with each key child? Is it every time the child attends the setting?	**13** How do you support children's transitions between Key Person relationships in the setting when there are staff changes (because of room changes, staff leaving etc)?	**14** Who is the 'back-up' Key Person for each child for when the Key Person is away for breaks, courses, holiday and so on? Does every staff member know who they are 'back-up' Key Person to?
15 How do you help the setting feel familiar and comfortable for each child especially any new ones?	**16** When do you reflect on how your setting might feel to different parents and children? How is this achieved?	**17** How do you communicate with parents of your key children who are very busy and don't have time to talk?	**18** How do you support children to make relationships with other children and adults?

The Key Person Approach © Anita Soni and Sue Bristow 2012

1	2	3	4
5	6	7	8
9	A Key Person has special responsibilities for working with a small number of children, giving them the reassurance to feel safe and cared for and building relationships with their parents.		10
11	12	13	14
15	16	17	18

The Key Person Approach © Anita Soni and Sue Bristow 2012

Scenarios for staff discussion

You can't have a Key Person approach in an out-of-school care setting because the child already has a Key Person in their Reception or nursery class.

Zoe has a Key Person, Miss Smith, in her nursery class. Zoe has built a warm relationship with Miss Smith in nursery, but now needs to go to the out-of-school club because her Mum is working longer hours. Does Zoe need a new Key Person in the out-of-school club?

Questions to consider

? Can a child have more than one Key person in their life?

? Does a child need a Key Person in every part of their life?

You can't have a Key Person approach in an out-of-school setting because it would involve staff writing observations and individual learning journey books for each child in the Foundation Stage.

Nathaniel is attending an out-of-school club after attending his Reception class. His teacher, Mr Patel, is keeping a learning journey for Nathaniel. Does Nathaniel need another Key Person as well as Mr Patel? Does he need another learning journey?

Questions to consider

? Can a child have more than one Key Person in their life?

? Does a child need a Key person in every part of his life?

? Does a child need a learning journey and observations collated by his Key person from his out-of-school club?

You can't have a Key Person approach as it worries the parents that their child may become more attached to their Key Person than to them as parents.

Maisie has recently started going to Selina, a childminder, and has settled in well. However Maisie has now started to cry when her parents come to collect her at the end of the day to take her home. This is worrying Maisie's mum who doesn't like to see her daughter getting upset.

Questions to consider

? Can a child have a close relationship with her Key Person and her parents?

? Can a Key Person build a relationship with a child without building a relationship with the child's parents?

You can't have a Key Person approach because practitioners may become over-attached to their key children.

Jamie has been in Toddlers for six months. He has a warm positive relationship with his Key Person, Danielle. Jamie is very keen to be with Danielle and gets upset when Danielle takes her lunch break. Danielle tends to cut her lunch short so that she can calm Jamie down. In addition Danielle is not keen to attend courses. While she realises that the courses may be helpful and give her further ideas on working with the toddlers, she worries that Jamie will get upset without her and other staff won't know how to comfort him.

Questions to consider

? Can a Key Person be effective without a supportive manager and support systems such as regular supervision?

? Is it fair on practitioners and children to have a Key Person approach without a 'back-up' Key Person approach?

You can't have a Key Person approach because the child may become too dependent on their Key Person.

Lila has been in the Baby room for four weeks. She bonded well with Richard her Key Person. Lila is very keen to be with Richard and gets upset when Richard is with other children or goes out of the room. Richard is a new practitioner in the Baby room and finds Lila quite demanding at times.

Questions to consider

? Can a Key Person be effective without a supportive manager and support systems such as regular supervision?

? Is it fair on practitioners and children to have a Key Person approach without a 'back-up' Key Person approach?

? Can a Key Person build a relationship with a child without building a relationship with the child's parents?

You can't have a Key Person approach as children become attached to their Key Person but still have to move to new rooms or new settings.

Jasmine attends the mixed-age playgroup, Busy Fingers, and is only going to be there for a year. This is unlike other children who attend for two or more years. The manager and staff are discussing whether Jasmine needs a Key Person as she seems very confident and is one of the oldest children at nearly four. She is due to go to Reception after spending her year in Busy Fingers.

Questions to consider

? Can a child have more than one Key person in their life?

? Does a child need a Key Person in every part of their life?

You can't have a Key Person approach because there is no way you can be there all the time for your key children – you may not be working when they arrive in the morning or you may have gone home from your shift when they go home at night.

Alisha attends a day nursery, Happy People, and does long hours on the three days she attends due her parents' work shifts as nurses and the distance they travel to work. Alisha arrives at nursery at 7.30am and leaves at 6pm. Her Key Person Sally does the morning shift and is there to open the nursery at 7.15am and finishes work at 3pm each day. Alisha has been at the nursery for a couple of weeks and is still a little unsettled.

Questions to consider

- Can a child have more than one Key Person in their life?

- Is it fair on practitioners and children to have a Key Person approach without a 'back-up' Key Person?

- Can a Key Person build a relationship with a child without building a relationship with the child's parents?

You can't have a Key Person approach as you have to work as part of a team and otherwise practitioners may say 'That's not my key child so I am not changing their nappy'.

Zane attends a set-up and pack-away playgroup, Jellytots, in the local church hall. He has developed a good relationship with Leah and is happy to attend playgroup. There have been a few staffing changes as a couple of staff have left and one long-standing member of staff has gone on maternity leave. The new members of staff are not familiar with the Key Person approach and have used a rotation approach for care routines. They believe that the children should learn to get along with everyone.

Questions to consider

- Can a child have more than one Key Person in their life?

- Does a child need a Key Person in every part of his life?

You can't have a Key Person approach in Reception because there are too many children and the children have to get ready for Year 1.

Jameel is about to start his second term in Reception class and turned five years old in October. He is in a class of 30. His previous teacher, Mrs Wills, has left for a new job. The teaching assistant, Miss Smith, has stayed with the class. A new teacher, Mrs Carr is taking over the class in January and is discussing with the Foundation Stage Coordinator and the teaching assistant whether it is worth allocating the children to a new Key Person as they have only got seven months in Reception before they move into Year 1.

Questions to consider

? Does a child need a Key Person in every part of his life?

? Does a child in Reception need a Key Person?

You can't have a Key Person approach because practitioners shouldn't have special children and should treat children all the same.

Natysha is in Marianne's key group and has been for some time. Marianne has a close relationship with Natysha and knows Natysha's mum very well. Another practitioner, Tanya, in the same room feels that Marianne favours Natysha over other children, fussing over her and keeping her on her knee for too long and not allowing her to explore. Tanya takes the issue up with her manager and says she feels the Key Person system is promoting staff favouring certain children.

Questions to consider

? Can a Key Person be effective without a supportive manager and support systems such as regular supervision?

? Is it fair on practitioners and children to have a Key Person approach without a 'back-up' Key Person?

? Can a Key Person build a relationship with a child without building a relationship with the child's parents?